Advance Praise for

The Inner Philosopher

In this day and age, when uncertainty reigns along with various other dictates that challenge all aspects of human endeavor, it is essential that *The Inner Philosopher* become a part of world literature and world dialogue. The content within takes one to the front lines of life's grand adventure of the enigmatic human condition and further on to an open and revealing dialogue, unraveling the mystery of "us."

> —Wayne Shorter, jazz composer and saxophonist, nine-time Grammy Award recipient, and National Endowment of the Arts Jazz Master

These sparkling and engaging conversations make a compelling case for the importance of philosophy in our lives and in our world. Daisaku Ikeda and Lou Marinoff are ideal guides to the nature and function of wisdom, from the times of the ancients through the challenges we all face now. This is a book that should be read by leaders, teachers, students, and adults of all ages.

> — Tom Morris, author of *Philosophy for Dummies*, *If Aristotle Ran General Motors*, and *If Harry Potter Ran General Electric*

In this exhilarating dialogue, Daisaku Ikeda and Lou Marinoff demonstrate the enormous power of practical, engaged philosophy. They inspire their readers to break the bonds of authority in order to develop their own inner resources—to embrace even the most difficult of life's questions with intellectual and emotional honesty, courage, discipline, and generosity.

> — Larry A. Hickman, Center for Dewey Studies, Southern Illinois University Carbondale

Do not pick up this book without a highlighter in your hand! You will want to return to many individual statements. Better still, plan a reading schedule to allow for each conversation, time to let the book drop into your lap while you ruminate on the most recently read of portions that will call you to do so. These conversations between Lou Marinoff and Daisaku Ikeda are rife with simple sentences that articulate shimmering complexities that light up the mind and move the reader to the contemplative reflection that is the medium of philosophy. Each exchange offers multiple keys to the doors of the reader's "inner philosopher."

These conversations illustrate that authentic truth seeking is a perennial characteristic of human thought; that knowledge is not a commodity to be monopolized by the powerful. We are instructed that philosophy begins with questions, a point congenial to peace educators who embrace critical pedagogy as a means through which to guide students toward what Daisaku Ikeda refers to as creating value; echoing what the educators see as peace building.

The open inquiry fundamental to peace education is brought to mind by Lou Marinoff's assertion that no one controls truth. The conversations invite all to be seekers of truth, assuring us that all can and should engage in philosophic reflection on the issues of our individual lives and our common society. We are encouraged by the wisdom the two share with each other and with us to release the inner philosopher to liberate the outer social actor. The book is a good "peace read."

— Betty A. Reardon, Founding Director Emerita,
International Institute on Peace Education

The Inner Philosopher

The Inner Philosopher

Conversations on Philosophy's Transformative Power

LOU MARINOFF

DAISAKU IKEDA

Dialogue Path Press
Cambridge, Massachusetts
2012

Published by Dialogue Path Press
Ikeda Center for Peace, Learning, and Dialogue
396 Harvard Street
Cambridge, Massachusetts 02138

Cover design by Schwadesign, Inc.
Interior design by Gopa & Ted2, Inc., and Eric Edstam

ISBN: 978-1-887917-09-4

Library of Congress Cataloging-in-Publication Data

Marinoff, Lou.
  [Tetsugaku runesansu no taiwa. English]
  The inner philosopher : conversations on philosophy's
transformative power / Lou Marinoff, Daisaku Ikeda.
    p. cm.
  Includes bibliographical references and index.
  ISBN 978-1-887917-09-4 (alk. paper)
  1. Conduct of life. 2. Buddhist philosophy. I. Ikeda, Daisaku. II. Title.
  BJ1595.M2565313 2012
  101—dc23

                                              2012002048

10 9 8 7 6 5 4 3 2 1

About Dialogue Path Press

Dialogue Path Press is the publishing arm of the Ikeda Center for Peace, Learning, and Dialogue, and is dedicated to publishing titles that will foster cross-cultural dialogue and greater human flourishing in the years to come. Prior to the founding of Dialogue Path Press, the center developed and published books in collaboration with publishers such as Orbis Books, Teachers College Press, and Wisdom Publications. These books, which focus on topics in education and global ethics, have been used in more than 800 college and university courses to date (2012). *The Inner Philosopher: Conversations on Philosophy's Transformative Power* is the third title published by Dialogue Path Press, following *Into Full Flower: Making Peace Cultures Happen* in 2010 and *Creating Waldens: An East-West Conversation on the American Renaissance* in 2009.

About the Ikeda Center

The Ikeda Center for Peace, Learning, and Dialogue is a nonprofit institute founded by Buddhist thinker and leader Daisaku Ikeda in 1993. Located in Cambridge, Massachusetts, the center engages diverse scholars, activists, and social innovators in the search for the ideas and solutions that will assist in the peaceful evolution of humanity. Ikeda Center programs include public forums and scholarly seminars that are organized collaboratively and offer a range of perspectives on key issues in global ethics. The center was originally called the Boston Research Center for the 21st Century and became the Ikeda Center in 2009.

For more information, visit the Ikeda Center website: www.ikedacenter.org

Table of Contents

Lou Marinoff and Daisaku Ikeda, Tokyo, 2003

CONVERSATION ONE

Philosophy Begins With Questioning

IKEDA: It's a tremendous honor to begin this dialogue[1] with you, Dr. Marinoff, a great philosopher of action who has brought fresh ideas and approaches to the world of philosophy.

Please let me thank you again for your sincere message in January 2008 on my eightieth birthday.

MARINOFF: You are more than welcome, President Ikeda. As I said in that message, you have done more in your eighty years than most of us could accomplish in eighty lifetimes. You have founded universities and a school system, established music societies and culture centers. You have published books and dialogues, inspiring people to live more wonderful lives than they ever dared to dream.

You are also a relentless Socratic inquirer after the truth. Your amazing accomplishments as an educator and a Buddhist of action are a beacon for all humankind. It is a signal honor for me to participate in a dialogue with you.

IKEDA: You praise me too highly.

It is no exaggeration to say that a lack of guiding philosophy is the basic cause of the impasse the world finds itself in today. A society without philosophy is like a building without a sound structure. No matter how splendid and richly ornamented its exterior, such a building, when battered by storms and earthquakes, must inevitably collapse. I cannot help thinking that the prosperity of modern civilization is equally fragile.

MARINOFF: I agree wholeheartedly with your assessment that our contemporary world suffers terribly from a lack of philosophy. Only when our vital forces are consecrated to probing life's deepest mysteries will our fuller human potential be activated.

IKEDA: Very true. Now is the time to unleash humanity's latent powers. From a society without philosophy emerges education without philosophy, which in turn gives rise to human beings with no philosophy, a dark portent for the future of humanity.

The twenty-first century must be a century of education and philosophy, thus becoming a century of life. I hope this dialogue will be a new departure for making it so.

You are a pioneer in making philosophy, which many people consider difficult and remote, easy to understand. I hope we can agree to proceed with the most accessible language possible.

MARINOFF: Yes, I do agree. Our challenge is to reclaim philosophy from the hands of the pure theoreticians—whose cogitations are abundant but whose applications are scarce—and return it to ordinary people. I intend to devote my best to this dialogue, with passion and spirit.

PHILOSOPHICAL COUNSELING

IKEDA: I am very happy to hear it. You have been an innovator in providing philosophical counseling and applying philosophies, old and new, Eastern and Western, to daily living, leading up to your founding of the American Philosophical Practitioners Association in 1998.

In Japan as elsewhere, people are showing a strong interest in counseling by psychotherapists and other specialized professionals to help them deal with a variety of challenges, including personal relationships, domestic difficulties, and problems in their social lives and interactions.

Counseling became popular in America at an early stage. However, the philosophical counseling that you are now pioneering is probably still unfamiliar to many. Could you explain it for our readers?

MARINOFF: In simple terms, in life we encounter various difficulties. To one extent or another, everyone worries, suffers, or feels disturbed. It has always been so. But when this happens in today's diagnostic cultures, people rely too heavily on psychiatry, psychology, and drugs. We philosophical practitioners strive to use wisdom traditions to convey alternative ways for people to think about and deal with their problems. Our goal is to awaken in our clients better conceptions of living, to help them confront their issues by manifesting their internal strengths.

IKEDA: That's one of the great values of philosophy. You've published many thought-provoking books on this topic, among which your *Plato, Not Prozac!* is a bestseller in many parts of the world.[2]

Prozac, of course, is the well-known antidepressant, while Plato here represents wisdom traditions. The book focuses on how we can deal with life's problems, arguing that by learning from the wisdom of philosophy, we can overcome the difficulties we encounter in life.

The purpose of philosophy, I believe, is to enable human beings to manifest their inner strength. One important means to do so is counseling—that is to say, guidance and dialogue. We of the Soka Gakkai International stress the importance of person-to-person dialogue based on the philosophy of respect for the dignity of life.

MARINOFF: The Soka Gakkai International's philosophy of life strikes me as very wholesome. Many of us within the APPA are becoming more aware of the role of dialogue in Buddhism and are implementing Buddhist approaches to dialogue with some of our clients.

As a teenager influenced by the 1960s counterculture movement, I became aware of Asian philosophies—Hinduism, Taoism, Buddhism—and by stages began to follow and incorporate their teachings in my life. I came to utilize philosophy as a guide for my own life for several decades, without ever intending to offer philosophical counseling to anyone else.

IKEDA: How did that change?

MARINOFF: In the early 1990s, I was working at the University of British Columbia's Centre for Applied Ethics in Vancouver, Canada. We applied ethicists found ourselves granting frequent media interviews—newspaper, radio, television—on numerous issues of social importance. But soon, members of the public began contacting the center on a regular basis, requesting philosophical advice on a variety of personal and professional matters.

They usually phoned in, asking to speak with a philosopher. That is how I got my first client: a high school principal who needed to resolve an ethical crisis. My second client was a walk-in: a graduate student at the university who sought advice on how best to care for his ailing mother while continuing his studies.

IKEDA: They were both facing serious problems. Can you share a little about the philosophical counseling you offered them?

MARINOFF: In the high school principal's case, we sought a resolution to a multiparty dispute based on moral rather than on legal grounds. Clashing legal opinions had only deepened the conflict, whereas an appeal to universal moral intuition largely resolved it. In the student's case, we sought to prioritize a number of distinct obligations, such that the student could fulfill them all successfully without compromising one duty for the sake of another.

IKEDA: In each case, you drew on philosophical tradition to suggest resolutions for the issue at hand.

MARINOFF: Yes. And I attempted to develop protocols for handling such cases. At the same time, it dawned on me that a significant public need was not being met, not even by Canada's universal health care and welfare-oriented social democracy. It became clear that some people need philosophers in their lives, at least at certain critical moments.

IKEDA: You responded to these needs with sincere action. You have been practicing philosophical counseling that, drawing on ancient and modern philosophy, gives people the wisdom and hope to resolve their problems.

No matter what the problem is, the way it is interpreted can have a positive or negative effect on one's life. By adopting a positive interpretation, one can make one's problems a source of nourishment for personal growth.

Regardless, using the powers of wisdom and dialogue to encourage and support people can be very challenging. At the same time, it is an extremely noble effort. Socrates, Plato, and Shakyamuni were all masters of such dialogue.

MARINOFF: Great masters indeed. Many enduring books from the ancient world were written as dialogues.

For me, philosophical counseling originates at the grass roots. It was started by citizens, not by philosophers. Ordinary people made the brilliant connection: since philosophy could address social issues, it could also address personal ones. So philosophical counseling emerged in response to public demand. That demand has grown worldwide in the ensuing years. My motivation, then and now, has been simply to respond with the conviction that I can help.

MANIFESTING OUR INHERENT NOBILITY

IKEDA: Starting at the grass roots—what a wonderful history!

No life is trouble-free. Everybody knows pain and suffering. Examined closely, even the apparently happy and carefree are often suffering within. Victor Hugo says, "As the life of even the most prosperous man is always in reality more sad than gay, a gloomy sky is in harmony with ourselves."[3]

In a sense, life is a series of hardships and sufferings. The important thing is finding a way to overcome them by changing each into an impetus for progress. When we can shift our viewpoint, we realize that troubles are the very things that help us grow as human beings. They are like fuel for the engine impelling us forward and upward.

A Buddhist doctrine teaches that earthly desires are the springboard to enlightenment. Only with the firewood of sufferings can we ignite the fire of wisdom and use it as the motivating force for achieving our happiness.

What is most important is learning how to convert the firewood of suffering into fuel for what we in the Soka Gakkai International call *human revolution*. That's where inquiry and practice based on a sound philosophy are indispensable.

MARINOFF: Buddhist doctrines are powerful and efficacious in helping people transform their suffering. These teachings need to be introduced more thoroughly to people who have been overexposed to psychology and ideology, and underexposed to philosophy.

I provide counsel to clients from virtually every walk and station of life. All of them share the desire to remedy their difficulties and to know the value, purpose, and meaning of their lives.

IKEDA: Consciously or unconsciously, everyone is seeking meaning and fulfillment in life. But no matter how hard one tries, these qualities cannot be found outside oneself. This is because the key lies only within. As the saying has it: "Dig where you stand. That's where you will find the spring."

It is truly noble how you use dialogue to illuminate people's innermost concerns and to send your clients a spring breeze of encouragement so that they can awaken to their inner strength and combat their difficulties.

MARINOFF: Thank you very much. In fact, this work has taught me that everyone is inherently noble. In my practice, the ultimate goal of dialogue is to help clients manifest their inherent nobility. This, in turn, enables them to work toward fulfillment with enhanced clarity, renewed energy, and enduring purpose.

Does this concept of philosophical counseling have a counterpart in Mahayana Buddhism?

IKEDA: Yes, it does. Mahayana Buddhism teaches giving as one of the bodhisattva practices.[4] There are three kinds of giving. The first two are to give material aid and to give the Law, or the teaching leading to enlightenment. Through the practice of giving, bodhisattvas fulfill their noble vow to aid all suffering people and help both themselves and others reach Buddhahood.

By extension, I think we can look at the provision of drugs and medicines by medical science as a form of material aid. There can be no denying the importance of drugs in combating diseases. The philosophical counseling that you offer is consonant with the spirit of giving the Law because you teach the pathway to happiness.

Another form of giving is the offering of fearlessness—that is, the elimination of people's dread and the provision of peace of mind. This gives people the courage to confront and overcome, ideally with absolutely no fear, hardships in business, daily life, and any area.

Mahayana Buddhism teaches that these kinds of giving make up the bodhisattva practice. Such must be the spirit of leaders and educators.

The aim of Buddhism is the achievement of a state free from all fears. It is a state in which each person, while manifesting supreme courage and peerless wisdom, strives for peace and the welfare of others.

MARINOFF: Your explanation of the bodhisattva practices is informative and illuminating, especially to Westerners, as it provides us with an ennobling rather than a stigmatizing context for dealing with life's anxieties. And doesn't Nichiren shed further light on this path?

IKEDA: As you know, Nichiren,[5] whose teachings we in the Soka Gakkai International follow, persistently emphasizes that difficulties refine and ennoble human beings:

> Difficulties will arise, and these are to be looked on as "peaceful" practices.[6]

> Only by defeating a powerful enemy can one prove one's real strength.[7]

> Iron, when heated in the flames and pounded, becomes a fine sword. Worthies and sages are tested by abuse.[8]

> Not to expect good times, but take the bad times for granted.[9]

Good Deeds In Everyday Life

MARINOFF: Wonderful words of inspiration! As understood in ancient Indian philosophy, an understanding continued by Buddhism, our greatest enemies are our own deluded mind-states and unrealistic expectations. Many Westerners have been lulled by affluence and indulgence into expecting lives free of all difficulty. Thus they have rendered themselves defenseless against the storm of existence. The teachings of Nichiren Buddhism offer a powerful refuge against this storm, yet many people are still unprepared to understand and practice them. People often require gradual instruction, step by step.

IKEDA: That's a universal principle, which I'm sure must apply to philosophical counseling as well.

As founder of both institutions, I thank you for attending the graduation ceremony for Soka University and Soka Women's College in Tokyo in March 2007. In my congratulatory speech at the ceremony, I took the liberty of introducing two points that you have made. Human beings, you have said, have the innate ability to make the best of adverse circumstances. And you have also asserted that a truly worthwhile, victorious life is one lived by overcoming suffering and creating value.[10]

After the ceremony, numerous students commented on how these points moved and encouraged them. Many of them continue to cherish your message in their post-graduation lives.

MARINOFF: I am happy to have exerted a positive influence on them. Proof of the true victory of humanity is the liberation of all people from suffering. This liberation is the goal of the Great Vehicle, Mahayana Buddhism. It means overcoming, not escaping, difficulty. People can achieve the best results in the worst circumstances but can become spoiled and heedless in fortunate conditions. They then grow insensitive to others' suffering, which in turn limits their own potential for spiritual growth.

In one of my works, I quote you on this topic: "Life is filled with truly unfathomable potential . . . in most cases, our so-called limitations are nothing more than our own decision to limit ourselves."[11] As you imply, human beings have the power to overcome their self-imposed limitations. Once we tear down our limitations, it becomes increasingly difficult for other people to shut us up within limiting walls.

IKEDA: Yes, it does. And we ourselves are the only ones who can tear down our limitations. In short, the individual human being is the standard and starting point of everything. Nichiren teaches, "Here a single individual has been used as an example, but the same thing applies equally to all living beings."[12]

A philosophy evoking passion, faith, and hope is required for each individual's triumph. What's your definition of *philosophy*?

MARINOFF: Philosophy is the love of wisdom. However, many people are afraid of philosophy, and with some justification, associating it with legendarily difficult mental exertions. The most esoteric ideas of theoretical philosophy—like those of theoretical physics and pure mathematics—are fully grasped by relatively few.

But at the same time, philosophy has always had a practical dimension as well as a theoretical one, and its practical applications are accessible to the vast majority of people. Aristotle, arguably the most influential philosopher in Western civilization, gives priority to practical wisdom.

For example, he says that people do not become good solely by contemplating goodness (as Plato would have us do) but more importantly by practicing goodness—that is, by doing good deeds in everyday life. So for Aristotle (as for many other practical philosophers), philosophy really means two things: contemplating wisdom and practicing ways of living wisely.

QUESTIONS ENLARGE OUR LIVES

IKEDA: And you are advocating this practical wisdom—or practical philosophy. The English word *philosophy* derives from the Greek word *philosophia*, which means love (*philos*) and wisdom (*sophia*). During the Meiji period (1867–1912), the Japanese philosopher Nishi Amane translated the term into Japanese as *tetsugaku*, employing the character *tetsu*, meaning "wisdom," and the character *gaku*, or "learning." Thus, *tetsugaku* means "study of wisdom."

How would you differentiate philosophy from ideology?

MARINOFF: Philosophy begins with questioning aimed at understanding and discovering truth. Instead of believing, it casts doubts.

Ideology, on the other hand, is founded on certainty, or even dogmatic inflexibility, about one's beliefs or the things one has been taught. Ideology can brainwash people, paralyzing their capacity to question.

IKEDA: Clearly put. Socrates strove to awaken his dialogue partners to truth by posing questions. One of your recent books is appropriately titled *The Big Questions*. An age without a guiding philosophy is an age in which people have forgotten to question. As you say, philosophy begins with questioning: the bigger the questions, the more profound the quest. Questioning enlarges our lives.

Great efforts and great achievements are possible precisely when big questions are asked. Perhaps to be truly human is to pursue a lifelong quest, risking everything, to answer the big questions.

Indolence generates no big questions. These questions, which make life more profound, arise when we face trials and difficulties directly instead of trying to evade them.

MARINOFF: This is very true. The great existential philosopher Nietzsche writes, "Man is a rope stretched . . . over an abyss."[13] That abyss yawns beneath everyone's feet, although many never realize this until they fall into it. Then, as you say, they are obliged to ask the big questions.

What were your formative philosophical influences? Who encouraged you to ask the big questions?

IKEDA: It would be impossible to discuss my life without mentioning my mentor, second Soka Gakkai president Josei Toda. I owe everything I am today to him. My life's mission has been to realize his ardent wishes for the happiness of all people and for peace. Toda was a compassionate educator and Buddhist—a popular leader who gave people limitless hope and courage. He thoroughly grasped the essential nature of philosophy and explained it to ordinary people in easy-to-understand ways.

My mentor once said:

> Philosophy isn't as complicated or hard to understand as Descartes or Kant. Some may say they don't know anything about philosophy because they didn't go to university, but to philosophize is simply to think.
>
> One basic example of philosophy can be found in the [fictional account of the travels] of Mito Mitsukuni [a feudal-period lord who traveled throughout Japan in disguise, righting wrongs and defending the helpless]. During his travels, he once asked an old peasant woman for some water and then sat down on a bale of rice. The woman, not recognizing who he was, flew into a rage, saying that

he was sitting on a bale of rice that was to go to Lord Mito. Abashed, Lord Mito bowed his head and apologized.

It was an ironic situation, of course, but for the old peasant woman, proudly offering this rice she had carefully harvested to the lord of her domain was her philosophy.

Philosophy comes down to standing up for the principles you believe in, no matter what.[14]

MARINOFF: This is a wonderful illustration, both humorous and serious at the same time. You were fortunate to have had such a sagacious mentor in Toda. Now I can better appreciate the source of your enduring and admirable commitment to practical philosophy.

IKEDA: We shouldn't look at philosophy or learning as mere trappings we don to make ourselves appear cultivated. Nor should we think of philosophy as something divorced from our lives or as the exclusive property of professional philosophers. Philosophy is for all serious, sincere people, regardless of their place in society or level of formal education. True philosophy thrives in the actions of every individual who tries to lead a good and honest life, unswayed by the temptations of fame or fortune. In this sense, your practical efforts, Dr. Marinoff, to return philosophy to the ordinary people and apply it broadly in daily life are sure to become a great light of hope illuminating the future of humanity.

Gratitude to Our Parents

IKEDA: You have helped overturn the long-standing impression that philosophical writings are always difficult and inaccessible. Already a best-selling author, you recently published *The Middle Way: Finding Happiness In a World of Extremes*,[1] which readers in many countries are enjoying. Your application of the traditional wisdom of moderation—drawn from Aristotelianism, Buddhism, and Confucianism, which you call the "ABCs" of virtue ethics—to the diverse problems of modern society is attracting serious attention from thoughtful readers.

MARINOFF: Thank you for your salient introduction of the key issues that *The Middle Way* addresses. I have quoted you as a leading exemplar, teacher, and innovator in the Mahayana Buddhist tradition throughout the book.

A variety of leaders in the global village are reading *The Middle Way*, and I hope it will influence them for the better. To be sure, it has helped many ordinary citizens better understand and help resolve the tensions in our global village. As we have already observed, much can be accomplished from the grass roots.

IKEDA: I believe that the idea of the Middle Way will have increasing significance in creating a society in which humanity can live in harmony and symbiosis.

A single book can exert immeasurable influence. Its ideas can transcend both time and space, changing the way people think around the world and through the ages. I hope our current dialogue will also greatly encourage and hearten people around the world now and in the future.

In this conversation, let's address the theme of family education and your recollections of your parents. I understand that your father, who loved art and literature, died when you were fifteen. Confronting his death must have been extremely painful for you. What are some of your most cherished memories of your father?

MARINOFF: My father's life, as well as his death, greatly influenced my appreciation of scholarly pursuits and a life devoted to learning. An intelligent man who lived a difficult and relatively short life, he never had the opportunity for higher education. That did not prevent him, however, from acquiring a strong taste for literature, poetry, philosophy, psychology, art, sports, music, and chess. He read copiously and imbued me at an early age with his keen appreciation of cultural pursuits.

My father also worked hard to pay my tuition to private school, which lay almost beyond his modest means. He sacrificed a great deal to confer on me the benefits of a privileged education, which he himself had been denied. I owe him an incalculable debt.

GRATEFUL AWARENESS OF OTHERS

IKEDA: I am touched by the depth of your beautiful gratitude and sense of indebtedness to your father. Living in grateful awareness of how we have benefitted from others—with the desire to make recompense—enriches our lives. Ignoring what we owe others closes the path to our personal growth. I always impress on young people the importance of respecting and caring for their parents.

As is clear from your example, gratitude toward our parents, while it may seem a small thing, is proof of our development and growth as human beings. My mentor was strict about people failing to appreciate their parents and treat them with consideration and respect. I still remember how he sharply rebuked one young man who had distressed his parents: "You should know how you make your parents cry!"

Toda said that "a person incapable of being a good son or daughter can never become happy or great." He also insisted that "a person who cannot love his parents can love no one. The essence of human revolution is overcoming our lack of compassion."

MARINOFF: That is certainly true. East and West converge on this point. Confucian cultures emphasize filial piety, while the Judeo-Christian tradition teaches the commandments of Moses that include "Honor your father and mother." Where children stop honoring their parents, society disintegrates.

Although we each have only one biological father, there are many other father figures in the form of mentors and sages. If we open our minds to such figures, we are certain to encounter lifelong guidance, such as you received from Toda.

Although my father is buried in a Jewish cemetery, his tombstone bears an inscription from the *Rubáiyát of Omar Khayyám*, his favorite Persian poet: "I came like Water, and like Wind I go."[2]

IKEDA: Your father was obviously a man with an open mind and heart who lived an exemplary life. Though time goes by like flowing water and moves ahead like the wind, I am sure that your fondly remembered father watches over you. He lives in your heart. I am confident that he would be happy to see you using philosophy to bring healing hope to countless people. In this sense, your triumph is his as well.

MARINOFF: Thank you for creating this opportunity for such heartfelt reminiscence. I am sure that my father would be very proud indeed to see that his tremendous sacrifices were not in vain and that they have borne helpful philosophical fruit for many people around the world. As you say, this is his triumph, for in doing my work I daily honor his memory.

IKEDA: What encouragement and advice do you have for young people who have lost their parents?

MARINOFF: To children and young adults who have lost their parents, I would suggest that one's parents are never truly departed. Their wisdom and virtue persist in the lives and deeds of their children and grandchildren.

Parents are guides who create our original path for lifelong learning. We must have the courage to follow that path, wherever it leads, and be grateful when other guides appear from time to time. Didn't Confucius say that he regarded all men as his instructors?

IKEDA: Yes, he did. In the *Analects*, there is the statement "When I walk with two others, I am bound to find my teacher there."[3] I am reminded of the celebrated Japanese novelist Eiji Yoshikawa's belief that everyone was his mentor, an attitude that expresses a humble willingness to keep learning.

People who are always eager to learn and develop, no matter their age or status, can manifest unlimited potential. In being modest and willing to grow, people add luster to the precious spiritual jewel inherited from their parents. This is another way that we can keep our parents alive in our hearts and ever-present in our lives, I believe.

Incidentally, I understand that your grandfather and grandmother, too, were fine people.

MARINOFF: They were hardworking and forthright people and imparted many virtues to their children and grandchildren. They escaped a life of great hardship and persecution in Russia, pursuing liberty, security, and opportunity in North America. Happily married for fifty-seven years, until my grandfather died, they lived for the future of their children and grandchildren. This is very important. We educators, too, must understand that children are beings of the future.

IKEDA: All children are emissaries from the future. All adults, not just parents, need to take responsibility for the future of our children.

I make it a rule to treat each child I encounter as an independent personality. Society would be more richly humane if we all thought and acted to give preeminence to the happiness of these "beings of the future." That is why I stress a shift from education that serves society's needs to a society that serves the essential needs of education.

To return to your family, I understand that your mother is still in good health. That is wonderful.

A MOTHER WHO ENCOURAGES CREATIVITY

MARINOFF: Yes, she is a strongly spiritual person who, in her late eighties, still writes inspiring poetry. My father and mother complemented each other well. He emphasized discipline; she encouraged creativity.

My father's emphasis on discipline taught me the virtue and value of hard work, practice, and perseverance. He hoped that I would aspire to a profession such as medicine or law, which no doubt he would have done if he had been afforded the opportunity. So he inculcated in me many virtues of professionalism.

My mother's encouragement prompted me to learn painting, music, poetry, and public speaking. She recognized more clearly that I was not going to follow a predefined path. My mother understood that I was gifted with creative energy and independence of mind—hallmarks of a philosopher.

These gifts were a source of pride but also of concern to my parents, who at times could not imagine what was to become of me. Even so, I was fortunate to have grown up during the golden age of capitalism, when the middle class flourished, and to have been blessed with a family that afforded me every opportunity to develop my capacities and encouraged me to pursue my interests.

IKEDA: The way your parents complemented each other suggests an ideal relationship.

Toda, by the way, was a brilliant educator and mathematician. Before World War II, he wrote his best-selling *Suirishiki shido sanjutsu* (A Deductive Guide to Arithmetic, published in 1930), which sold more than a million copies.

He gave me much advice on family education, including the following:

> Because a mother's anger comes from a mother's love, her strictest scolding has no ill effect but only makes children reflect more on their behavior. A father's reprimands, by contrast, can seem coldhearted and actually push children in the direction of trouble.

Toda said that a father and mother should not scold their children at the same time, making them feel cornered with no refuge.

He encouraged parents to "see their children off to school with a wave" and "telephone them often when a busy schedule requires frequent trips away." Toda believed that "children should be allowed freedom, but parents should always be aware of what they are doing and keep an eye on them."

His advice was subtle and sensitive. Small, spontaneous demonstrations of caring, after all, can have a huge effect on children and family life in general. Each point of his advice became indescribable support for my wife and me. He gave straightforward advice from the perspective of Nichiren Buddhism. To this day, I feel a debt of deep gratitude to my mentor.

Children are always observing their parents and can be deeply wounded by their quarrelling. It is most important for parents to complement and aid each other in creating a wise, cheerful home where the children can grow freely.

Can you share when your family went through its most difficult times?

War, Cruel and Barbarous

MARINOFF: All families are heir to episodes of suffering and strife, and ours was no exception. World War II touched all our immediate relatives. My mother's only brother, an aviator who had great talent and promise as a writer, was killed in Europe. My father served with the Canadian ground forces that helped liberate North Africa, France, and Italy from Nazi occupation. When he learned of the Holocaust, he decided to assist in the rebirth of the State of Israel and joined its provisional defense force, the Haganah, in 1947. The severe wounds he received in Israel's War of Independence—the Arab-Israeli War of 1948, not long after World War II—shortened my father's life considerably.

Even so, my parents bestowed on me not only the gift of life but moreover a happy, sunlit childhood and a resplendently idyllic boyhood. They helped prepare me for a difficult coming-of-age and for future challenges that my mother presciently foresaw and that my father (had he lived) would have been proud to see me take up.

Most of humanity was shaken by the calamities of World War II and still suffers from problems spawned in its aftermath. I believe the war had serious effects on you and your family, too.

IKEDA: Yes, it did. Nothing is as cruel and barbarous as war.

My friend Mikhail S. Gorbachev and I have met numerous times, become close friends over the years, and published together *Moral Lessons of the Twentieth Century*. In this dialogue, he emphasizes: "We were wartime children who survived. Nothing of the life and deeds of our generation is understandable unless we take this into consideration."[4]

The war damaged our entire youth. All four of my brothers were drafted one after another in the prime of their lives.

My father was stricken with rheumatism at that time. Thus from my mid-teens, I became the chief breadwinner. I went to work in a munitions plant, even though I had tuberculosis and was frequently coughing up blood.

Sometimes air raids sent us fleeing for our lives amid the flames. After our old house was destroyed, we built a new one in what we thought was a safer area. But to our great distress, it also burned down in an air raid just one day before we were to move in.

Among the countless young lives lost in the war was that of my oldest brother, who died on a battlefield in Burma (now Myanmar) at twenty-nine. My mother and father believed he would come home safe until, in May 1947, two years after the war ended, they received official notification of his death. I will never forget how my mother—ordinarily a strong, cheerful woman—shook with grief.

I oppose all war, no matter what reasons are advanced to justify it. These family experiences served as the nucleus of my subsequent antiwar and pacifist actions. In war, it is the ordinary people, the least powerful people—especially women, including mothers—who suffer the most. We must eradicate this tragedy from the world.

Regarding his debt to his mother and his vow to serve the people, Nichiren writes:

> Since I have realized that only the Lotus Sutra teaches the attainment of Buddhahood by women, and that only the Lotus is the sutra of true requital for repaying the kindness of our mother, in order to repay my debt to my mother, I have vowed to enable all women to chant the daimoku [in other words, Nam-myoho-renge-kyo] of this sutra.[5]

I believe that respect for women and the human impulse to demonstrate our gratitude to our mothers are two essential components of a philosophy that aims to create a peaceful, symbiotic world.

THE POWER OF GOOD WOMEN

MARINOFF: As I write in *The Middle Way*, women's powers must be fully developed. Achieving this demands equality of opportunities. Of course, such equality cannot resolve all issues, since equality of opportunities will always lead to unequal outcomes. The important thing is harmony between the sexes.

In a sense, it is harder being a woman than being a man. Many of the women who come to me for counseling say that they want to bear and raise children, but they also want to succeed in their professional careers. Doing all this at the same time is difficult. Right now, we are in the midst of various large-scale socio-political experiments in this area. No one can foresee all the consequences of the social engineering taking place.

IKEDA: Creating a more caring, supportive society is inseparably connected with creating an environment in which women feel free both to have families and to be active in society. That is why we must pool our wisdom and strive even more earnestly to create a social system that includes greater participation by women.

Traditionally, most societies have been male-centered and have failed to fully utilize women's distinctive characteristics and wisdom. But the ideal feminine traits of a sense of justice, compassion for life, love of peace, and talent for strengthening human bonds can effect great changes in today's cruel, violence-ravaged world. Deliberately including and getting the most out of their flexible wisdom and sensitivity can give new vitality to society.

Ralph Waldo Emerson, in praising women's flair for "wise, cultivated, genial conversation," writes that "women are, by this and their social influence, the civilizers of mankind. What is civilization? I answer, the power of good women."[6]

I hope we can later discuss from many angles the role of women and the optimum future society (see Conversation Fifteen).

Calling Forth the "Inner Philosopher"

IKEDA: You are the chairman of the Philosophy Department at The City College of New York, flagship college of The City University of New York. The founder of your college was Townsend Harris, the first US consul-general to Japan. He arrived in Japan in 1856 and helped open the country to the world.

City College was formerly known as the Free Academy of the City of New York, founded in 1847. The college was open to all people. It has not been well known in Japan that Harris devoted himself wholeheartedly to its founding.

MARINOFF: The Townsend Harris Hall, named after him, stands magnificently on the campus today, and the library houses his journals and public papers, as well as an American flag that once flew over the consulate general in Shimoda, Japan.

IKEDA: Harris's educational philosophy was that the doors of education should be open to everybody. His efforts for the people's happiness and for social improvement through education demonstrated his profound love for humanity.

At Soka University of Japan, we have had the spirit that "universities should exist for the sake of those who were unable to attend them." We have also worked to make Soka University open to anyone who wants to study by providing correspondence courses.

In a speech you once delivered at Soka University of America (in 2003), you said that the ideal university should be a place where good faculty and good students influence one another and learn together. This is a very important point. I am convinced that a humble spirit of learning together and a profound love for humanity must lie at the heart of any educational institution.

What do you think makes for a good professor?

MARINOFF: Learning is the first condition—keeping an open mind for the sake of learning. To be a good professor is to devote oneself to lifelong learning. We learn through our research and peer-reviewed publications; we learn from our colleagues; and perhaps above all, we learn from our students in the very process of teaching them. Time and again, I have discovered that teaching a course provides an invaluable way of deepening my own learning.

To share one of my teaching methods, let me refer to my Introduction to Philosophy course. I like teaching this course because most of the students do not yet know any philosophy, so they are quite excited by and amenable to inquiry. At the outset, I encourage each student to question. This is the reverse of the ordinary method, in which questioning follows instruction. But I say to them that, although I might give a foolish answer, there is no such thing as a foolish question. The important thing is questioning. This encourages them to ask.

IKEDA: That's a wonderful approach to teaching, and there's much we can learn from it. Education truly is an art.

The student's natural desire to learn cannot be tapped if the teacher insists on a unilateral teaching style aimed at little more than cramming facts into the student's head. Rather, teachers need to take their students' questions about the why and wherefore of things seriously and focus on fostering that inquisitive spirit. The teacher's role is to provide stimulation and encouragement, and to instill in students the confidence to take initiative in the pursuit of knowledge. This is the educator's great mission. A know-it-all, condescending disposition disqualifies a teacher as an educator. Your efforts to bring out students' natural curiosity and desire to learn, based on your openness to learning together with them, are a wonderful model for other educators to emulate.

LISTENING DEEPENS DIALOGUE

MARINOFF: From our dialogue so far, I get the impression that you use skillful questioning to call forth responses from others. In your wonderful ability to do this, you recall Socrates, who employed brilliant questions to get at the essence of things.

At the same time, you are an extremely good listener. The ability to listen is the quintessential way to prevent questioning from becoming interrogation. Listening to the other party deepens resonance and exchange, thus propelling dialogue forward.

IKEDA: Though it may seem passive, listening is in fact a creative way to generate positive dialogue. Buddhism teaches the supreme importance of listening: "This saha world [the world, which is full of suffering] is a land in which one gains the way through the faculty of hearing."[1] In a world flooded with information, a dialogue that is a mingling of voices and hearts is increasingly necessary.

MARINOFF: The sincere questioning I have heard from students at the Soka schools in Japan[2] and Soka University of America made a favorable impression on me. Their sharp questions indicate that they will grow into future philosophers.

Children, by the way, are emotionally more vulnerable to disparaging remarks than adults and are less capable of defending themselves against slights and other verbal abuse. Among the first duties of parents and teachers alike is encouragement of talents and correction of errors.

But the second of these duties is almost always most effectively accomplished in a climate of encouragement rather than disparagement. Therefore, we should begin by praising the child or the student with respect to whatever he or she is doing correctly and well.

As an avid student of classical guitar, I was fortunate to have studied privately with several great masters. Not one of them ever uttered a disparaging word to any of their students. No matter how poorly a student might play—and students would sometimes be overcome by nerves and fall apart—the master would always point out some beautiful aspect of the student's playing to use as a departure point for correcting serious flaws.

PRAISE THE POSITIVE

IKEDA: It is impossible to overstate the importance of praise and encouragement in fostering growth and character development. Especially today, I'd say it's important for leaders in all fields of endeavor to combine 20 percent leadership with 80 percent praise.

An authoritarian approach—forcing children to do as you say or to make them conform to certain preconceived standards—only provokes rebelliousness. Though you may succeed in gaining their superficial obedience, it's very difficult under those circumstances to enable children to freely manifest their full potential. As you show us, it's important for adults to continue learning together with children.

Your mention of music reminds me of something Pablo Casals once wisely said: "To teach is to learn."[3]

MARINOFF: I agree with him entirely. He was not only a gifted performer but also a legendary teacher.

IKEDA: Gregor Piatigorsky recalled having been so nervous when he played as a student for the great musician that he froze and performed badly. Afterward, however, Casals called out "Bravo! Bravo!" and, embracing him, praised his performance: "Wonderful! Great!" Convinced he had played poorly, Piatigorsky was perplexed by Casals's response.

Meeting Casals again years later, Piatigorsky confessed his confusion at Casals's reaction:

> [Casals] rushed to the cello. "Listen!" He played a phrase from the Beethoven sonata. "Didn't you play this fingering? Ah, you did! It was novel to me . . . it was good . . . and here, didn't you attack that passage with an up-bow, like this?" He demonstrated . . . . "And for the rest," he said passionately, "leave it to the ignorant and stupid who judge by counting only the faults. I can be grateful, and so must you be, for even one note, one wonderful phrase."[4]

It's very important to discover, encourage, and praise the positive aspects—even just one—of the generations who follow us. We must foster young people's confidence in themselves.

MARINOFF: My meetings with wonderful students at the Soka schools in Japan gave me a sense of the students' passion, spirit, hope, and high standards. I felt that they were the kind of youth to whom we can entrust the destiny of the world.

IKEDA: Thank you for saying so. As founder, I have devoted my utmost efforts to the Soka schools with the firm resolution and prayer to cultivate people who can make significant contributions to the world. That is why your words make me so happy. Graduates of Soka schools are already active all over the world.

A word of encouragement—as Casals demonstrated with his students—can have a decisive impact on a human life. Through your practical philosophy, you are shining a new light on the significance and importance of encouragement.

ENCOURAGE COMES FROM COURAGE

MARINOFF: Encouragement is an essential ingredient in realizing human potential. In this respect, my clients in philosophical counseling sessions resemble students in the classroom: they must be encouraged to inquire, to find the key that unlocks their inner resources. The root of *encourage* is *courage*—thus, *encouragement* means inspiring their courage.

In counseling, the most important words are eventually uttered by the clients themselves, once the power of dialogue unfetters their courage (among other virtues) and awakens their philosopher within. The clients' "inner philosopher" ultimately speaks the most significant words, which I then reflect back to them. At that moment, they no longer need me, for they can encourage themselves.

IKEDA: "Inner philosopher" is a wonderful expression concisely describing the power within each human life.

Helen Keller, who triumphed over a triple challenge (sight, speech, and hearing) to become a source of boundless courage and hope to others, writes, "Philosophy gives to the mind the prerogative of seeing truth, and bears us into a realm where I, who am blind, am not different from you who see."[5]

The ability to awaken in the breast of each individual this inner philosopher—to bring forth virtue and happiness from within—

embodies the profound meaning of dialogue and the challenge of practical philosophy.

The initial conversation in our dialogue (published in Japanese in *Pumpkin* magazine, June 2008) has already aroused great interest. One young reader is especially curious to know why you chose the path of philosophy after studying theoretical physics.

MARINOFF: My secondary education at Lower Canada College covered a classic curriculum spanning arts and sciences. After LCC, I studied liberal arts at Dawson College, studied and taught classical guitar, and performed music professionally in several idioms. I then took up theoretical physics, which employs elegant mathematical models to plumb the depths of the phenomenal world.

By stages, I came to appreciate connections among music, mathematics, and philosophy. I re-focused on philosophy because theoretical physics—however refined and beautiful—lacks moral content. I could not envision for myself a lifetime steeped in thought to the neglect or exclusion of qualitative (i.e., values-based) inquiry.

NOT FOR ONE'S BENEFIT ALONE

IKEDA: I respect your diligent research and achievements in ethics and values. The progress of ethics has not kept pace with the rapid progress of science. This is one of the tragedies of our times. Science run wild is epitomized by nuclear weapons, which jeopardize human existence.

In our dialogue *A Quest for Global Peace*, the famed physicist and devoted champion of nuclear disarmament Joseph Rotblat and I agreed that sound morals and philosophy must be the indispensable foundation of science and learning. To promote this,

Dr. Rotblat insisted that, after their intellectual training, all university graduates should take something like the Hippocratic oath. Dr. Arnold J. Toynbee, with whom I published the dialogue *Choose Life*, had a similar view. From this perspective, the role of practical philosophy, which aims to elevate our lives by implementing the wisdom of the philosophical tradition, will become increasingly important.

MARINOFF: Rotblat's idea is brilliant and necessary. Contemporary physicians still take the Hippocratic oath ceremonially (even though parts of it are outmoded by modern science) to bear in mind a fundamental and unchanging ethical precept: medicine is practiced primarily to help others and not to advantage oneself. Similarly, while we at LCC were beneficiaries of a privileged education, the school's motto was *"Non nobis solum,"* meaning "Not for ourselves alone." So I thoroughly endorse Rotblat's idea. Everyone who receives a higher education must appreciate that such a gift is intended to benefit humanity.

IKEDA: Yes, without question. Your own path of study has been incredibly diverse, ranging from music to physics and philosophy. I imagine that all of your interests arose fundamentally from your interest in humanity.

MARINOFF: It is all for the sake of understanding human beings, exploring the incredible powers of the human mind, and addressing the perennial need for humanistic ethics. As the saying goes, "The blind cannot lead the blind." So we must develop our own resources in order to understand and be of service to others.

Now I should like to ask you some questions. The numerous books by you that I have read have filled me with admiration. How did you attain such profound understanding of so many different matters? You, too, must have learned by asking questions and engaging in discussion.

Ultimately Truth Triumphs

IKEDA: As I have said before, I owe everything to the instruction I received in my youth from my mentor. In the years following World War II, our values in Japan were in chaos. I was earnestly seeking a solid philosophy.

The summer two years after the war (1947), when I was nineteen, I met Toda. Despite being oppressed by the militarists and his two-year imprisonment, he had courageously remained true to his faith. From the moment of our first meeting, his personality attracted me. I immediately knew that he was a person I could trust.

Toda instructed me in a wide range of fields, including law, economics, literature, history, philosophy, and science. The personal instruction I received from him in my youth was absolutely life changing.

MARINOFF: I imagine that he instructed you through person-to-person dialogue.

IKEDA: Yes, it was incredibly stimulating and inspiring—a no-holds-barred encounter between two individuals at the deepest level.

Toda had fought resolutely against Japanese militarism and experienced life to the fullest. Each and every word he uttered revealed him to be a true master of life. Above all, he loved young people and was dedicated to fostering their growth and development.

I am distressed to observe a lamentable lack of this kind of affection for youth among many societal leaders today. Young people's minds are sensitive and cannot be cultivated by the egotistical and compassionless. We should treasure youth as our comrades in seeking truth and creating value.

The motto of the American Philosophical Practitioners Association is "Nobody governs truth." I have heard that this reflects your wish to liberate people from political and religious authority.

MARINOFF: Indeed, this motto is the APPA's answer to the burning question "Who governs truth?" As you say, it asserts that nobody has the authority to govern, dictate, legislate, or otherwise control truth. As human beings, we may be privileged to realize, discover, learn, or teach certain truths. But at the same time, we are governed by them, not they by us. Truth will always triumph in the end, though political and religious authorities may attempt to plunge humanity into darkness by clouding minds, disseminating propaganda, and persecuting truth-tellers.

This has been so in the past and remains so today. The philosopher loves truth. Nichiren was oppressed for pointing out the way to freedom for the masses. Socrates, Plato, and many other philosophers likewise encountered hardships in their pursuit of truth. Tsunesaburo Makiguchi,[6] founder with Toda of the Soka Gakkai, also followed a similar path.

IKEDA: Socrates was falsely accused and sentenced to death. Shakyamuni and Nichiren, too, were jealously defamed and slandered. It is often precisely because they are correct that great people are abused and oppressed. This has been the case throughout the history of human society in all parts of the world.

But the wise, just person never bows to oppression of any kind and considers persecution a mark of honor. Confrontation with difficulties only makes his or her philosophical approach deeper and more brilliant.

LEADERS MUST SERVE THE PEOPLE

MARINOFF: You have said that the proper role of leaders is to serve, and with this I concur wholeheartedly. Having conducted philosophy workshops for world leaders and retreats for future world leaders,[7] I have told them exactly the same thing, using two diagrams. The first diagram depicts a leader ensconced at the apex of a pyramid, presiding over increasingly broad subordinate layers of his organization and apparently enjoying a position of superiority and dominance. The second diagram depicts the same pyramid inverted, the apex facing downward and the leader at the bottom, bearing the weight and burden of the entire edifice. It portrays the proper role of the leader: not to exploit the people from above but to elevate them from below.

IKEDA: That is a very important point. For the sake of realizing a thoroughly democratic, humanistic society, we must transform—indeed, revolutionize—our ideas about leadership. Leaders must be imbued with the idea of supporting and serving the people, as in your second diagram, and take the initiative in putting this into practice. When this happens, society will change greatly.

Those who try to dominate and control the people are not genuine leaders. Neither are those who exploit the youth. They are, simply put, authoritarian. By contrast, true leaders accept all responsibility for supporting, guiding, and serving the people. Above all, leaders must be compassionate and love humanity deeply.

MARINOFF: You have created so much value and opportunity for so many others in your capacity as leader of the Soka Gakkai International. Having served so many for so long, you must have borne correspondingly enormous weight. How have you sustained the fortitude to bear such burdens of service?

IKEDA: Thank you for being so understanding. The mentor-disciple relationship that I learned through Toda has given me the strength to persevere in my work. My whole life has consisted of the unwavering determination to carry out the vow I made to Toda.

In the postwar ruins, Toda resolved to "banish the word *misery* from the face of the earth"[8] and fought for the happiness of the people with a fervor that consumed his life. As his disciple, I have devoted my life to making his cherished wish come true. No hardships have made me flinch. Indeed, they have only strengthened my resolve to fight on. Even today, morning and night, I constantly engage in a dialogue with Toda.

Day in, day out, I have worked, prayed, and hoped for the happiness and triumph of the Soka Gakkai International members. I have opened the way for youthful successors with the spirit of the oneness of mentor and disciple.

The happiness and triumph of all beings are the goals of Buddhism.

MARINOFF: I am touched by your determination and extend my sincere congratulations to you for making the Soka Gakkai International a driving force for worldwide peace, for creating value, and for improving the way of life of people in scores of countries. You are truly working for the happiness of all beings. Your life is a model for us all.

CONVERSATION FOUR

The Source of Robust Optimism

IKEDA: In the stress and anxiety of modern society, how can we learn to live more optimistically and hopefully? The time has come to ask ourselves how we can genuinely improve our psychological health in order to live more fully human lives.

How can philosophy and psychology make a positive contribution in times like these? You have said, from the standpoint of practical philosophy, that Freud and the psychoanalysts undervalued the strong, positive aspects of human nature, focusing instead on our negative aspects and weaknesses. Your point is very important.

Dr. Martin Seligman, a famous advocate of positive psychology and a former president of the American Psychological Association, sees things similarly. When we once met in Tokyo, he told me:

> Optimism is hope. It is not the absence of suffering. It is not always being happy and fulfilled. It is the conviction that though one may fail or have a painful experience somewhere, sometime, one can take action to change things.[1]

MARINOFF: Since you prefaced this conversation with a reference to psychology, especially the positive psychology of Seligman, allow me to answer in the same vein. Psychologists have discovered that optimism is a vital factor among shipwreck survivors, who are sometimes adrift on the ocean for days in open rafts, exposed to the elements and other hazards. Often they have inadequate food and water. Those who sustain a positive attitude and believe they will be rescued in time stand a better chance of surviving their ordeal than those who despair and give up hope.

This principle is true not only in drastic circumstances but also in daily life. We all know people who tend to emphasize the positive aspects of a given situation and others who tend to dwell on the negative ones. In ordinary situations, emphasizing the positive almost always brings better results than emphasizing the negative. In dire situations, it can spell the difference between life and death.

IKEDA: You make another important point. People react differently to the same circumstances according to their state of mind, and their lives then go in different directions. In the Soka Gakkai, we call this the person's "life-condition" or "life tendency."

Nichiren teaches:

> It is like the example of the Ganges River. Hungry spirits see the waters of the river as fire, human beings see them as water, and heavenly beings see them as amrita [liquid immortality]. The waters are the same in all cases, but each type of being sees them differently, according to the effects of its karma.[2]

The way one sees and responds emotionally to the world depends upon one's life-condition. From your extensive experience in philosophical counseling, I imagine that you must have seen this to be true.

MARINOFF: Yes, my experience has repeatedly confirmed this. Mind-states are influenced by such factors as brain chemistry, selective memory, psychological conditioning, and self-conception. Yet we can ennoble our mind-states and engender good outcomes regardless of circumstances; by exercise of will power, for example, which is underutilized in the West.

Aristotle writes, "We reply that if each man is somehow responsible for his state of mind, he will also be himself somehow responsible for the appearance."[3] He emphasizes that virtuous habits of thought conduce to a brightened mind.

BLESSINGS IN DISGUISE

IKEDA: If your mind shines, your life shines. Nichiren conveys this teaching from the Vimalakirti Sutra: "If the minds of living beings are impure, their land is also impure, but if their minds are pure, so is their land."[4] The mind is truly amazing. We must try to orient it in a positive direction, toward a life that creates value, and that's where practical philosophy can play a crucial role.

MARINOFF: And so the life-condition of practicing Buddhists tends to be correspondingly vibrant. We may ask, in the well-known Western metaphor, is the cup half empty or half full? Pessimists typically regard it as half empty; optimists, as half full.

To give a quotidian application of this metaphor, suppose that one is stuck in traffic and running late for an appointment. Pessimists will bemoan the traffic jam and complain that they are losing time. Optimists will typically say: How do you know that being stuck is not a blessing in disguise? Perhaps by being stuck

here and now, you avoid a terrible traffic accident awaiting you far-
ther along your route. According to the cabala, Judaism's esoteric
tradition, every situation can and should be interpreted positively
to celebrate each moment of existence.

IKEDA: That's a compelling example with profound implications.
In the most challenging circumstances, an optimistic outlook can
often alter reality and open the way to a brighter future. My mentor
used to say to young people, "Face life with a positive attitude!"

I'm reminded of a story that Gorbachev, who was pivotal in
bringing the Cold War to a close, told me about behind-the-scenes
events at one of his meetings with President Ronald Reagan. It was
in 1986 that Gorbachev and Reagan held their historic summit in
Reykjavik, Iceland. Unfortunately, while the world watched in an-
ticipation, the summit broke down. But at a press conference after
the meeting, Gorbachev carefully avoided saying it was a failure,
instead positioning it as the first step toward future discussions.

The American representatives had been publicly calling the
summit a failure, but when they heard Gorbachev's declaration,
they grasped his meaning and revised their stance, casting the
meeting's result in a more optimistic light. As history shows,
from that time on, the United States and the Soviet Union moved
steadily toward ending the Cold War.

A subtle shift in thinking can create opportunities with history-
making results. I think the same principle applies on the personal
level.

MARINOFF: What a fine example of the point we are illustrating.
By the way, I have read your dialogue with Gorbachev, and it is
outstanding. It should be required reading for anyone who seeks
to avoid repeating history's errors.

Returning to our point, by looking for the good in people and in circumstances, we find it. By contrast, we can always find something to complain about in our imperfect world, but that ruins the moment by disregarding what is good. The cabala and your example of the US-Soviet summit both illustrate the value of cultivating optimism.

INCORRIGIBLE OPTIMISTS

IKEDA: I admire your valuable efforts to continue sharing your philosophy of hope and optimism. Helen Keller writes that "optimism is the faith that leads to achievement; nothing can be done without hope."[5] She also writes, "We have seen that the world's philosophers—the Sayers of the Word—were optimists; so also are the men of action and achievement—the Doers of the Word."[6]

Mahatma Gandhi considered himself an incorrigible optimist. I think that many of the world's great achievers have been optimists in the true sense. This is true of Gorbachev, former South African president Nelson Mandela, and the environmentalist Wangari Maathai. Whether world leaders, scholars, or ordinary citizens, the majority of the great individuals I have met are incorrigible optimists.

MARINOFF: Keller, both deaf and blind at a time when people with physical disabilities were typically stigmatized and devalued, overcame not only her own challenges but also the handicapped perspectives held by her society.

I share your experience of encountering indefatigable optimism among highly accomplished people in every sphere. Great spirits remain unbroken in the face of adversity. Even calamity serves only to strengthen their resolve.

Surely you are also to be counted among the "incorrigibly optimistic." You have consistently encouraged only the most positive

aspirations for individuals and humanity as a whole. You have infused millions of Soka Gakkai International members with your
relentless optimism.

IKEDA: You praise me too generously.

Dr. Mihály Csíkszentmihályi, famous for his psychology of happiness,[7] is a friend of mine and very understanding of the Soka
Gakkai International and its work. One aspect of his research profoundly impressed me. From interviews he conducted, he discovered that many of the world's exemplary achievers share a number
of points in common: they are optimists, they are always open to
the future and the community, and they exhibit a deep sense of
responsibility and integrity in their lives.

MARINOFF: Based on my encounters with true world leaders —
whether in the political, commercial, religious, or cultural domains
—I concur with Csíkszentmihályi's view that they all manifest the
virtues of optimism, openness, truthfulness, and responsibility.

One can also observe the converse: the most terrible despots
tend to manifest the vices of pessimism, rigidity, untruthfulness,
and irresponsibility. What then is the significance of optimism
from a Buddhist perspective?

CONVERTING POISON INTO MEDICINE

IKEDA: I believe that true optimism is synonymous with absolute faith in human possibilities, unbending belief in our ability
to conquer all hardships, and the courage to strive continuously
to improve ourselves and the world around us. Buddhism teaches
that it is the self that transforms reality and creates new value.

It also teaches the principle of changing poison into medicine—
that when, through Buddhist practice based on the Mystic Law,[8]
one elevates one's life-condition, one can change the "poison" of

earthly desires and sufferings into "medicine": something positive for one's further personal growth and development. A firm belief in this principle, it seems to me, is the optimism that enables us to live to the fullest.

MARINOFF: Nagarjuna's teaching of converting poison into medicine is expressed in *The Treatise on the Great Perfection of Wisdom.*

IKEDA: And it was further developed by Zhiyi (also known as the Great Teacher Tiantai), founder of the Tiantai school in China, and Nichiren.

MARINOFF: From my association with you and your colleagues, I have come to appreciate this teaching more deeply. If we grant the all-important premise of free will, then insofar as thinking is habitual, negative interpretations of circumstances can be changed, over time and with some help, into positive ones.

Epictetus bequeathed us a pithy aphorism that has helped many people, including some of my clients, make cognitive breakthroughs into the realm of the positive: "Men are disturbed, not by Things, but by the Principles and Notions, which they form concerning things."[9] Is this not positive psychology plus positive philosophy in a nutshell?

IKEDA: Indeed. Changing one's view of things is the first step in revolutionizing the self and transforming one's environment.

Nichiren teaches, "The three obstacles and four devils will invariably appear, and the wise will rejoice while the foolish will retreat."[10] Problems and troubles are actually opportunities for significant personal change, a fact of which the wise are well aware. This is why Buddhism encourages people to face their difficulties joyfully and courageously.

When viewed from high in the heavens, the most violent waves seem no more than ripples. Our happiness greatly depends on establishing a strong life-condition from which we view events with that kind of serene equanimity.

MARINOFF: We cannot always or immediately alter our circumstances or indeed change brute facts. But we can always and immediately alter the views we take of them. This can make all the difference in the world.

OUR POTENTIAL LIMITLESS

IKEDA: Consequently, instead of being controlled by circumstances, we must have a viewpoint so firm that we can exert a mighty controlling influence on them. As John Milton writes in *Paradise Lost*, "The mind is its own place, and in itself Can make a Heaven of Hell, a Hell of Heaven."[11] Our minds determine our life's direction.

As the phrase "the wonderful workings of one mind"[12] implies, Buddhism offers a multidimensional examination of the limitless potential of the mind. We are in especially great need today of a philosophy, a way of thought, enabling us to direct our lives toward the shining sun of hope, peace, and happiness.

MARINOFF: As a practical philosophy, Buddhism unfailingly provides dissolution of obstructions to the inner light of mind. Milton (among other gifted Western poets and philosophers) rediscovered subtle properties of mind with which Buddhism had long been intimately acquainted. Buddhism offers more ways than any philosophy I know to activate human potential, to change life for the better, and to engender positive circumstances. More than ever, we need optimistic thinking in this twenty-first-century world.

IKEDA: Confronted as we are today with such huge problems as poverty, food shortages, environmental issues, and international conflicts, many people think it's impossible for the individual to make a difference and have succumbed to a feeling of impotence. The fact is, however, that the only way forward for humanity is for each of us to conquer this sense of powerlessness, tap our innate potential to the fullest, and work together in solidarity. I believe an optimism rooted in a higher order of spirituality is the source of the power we need to achieve these things.

Keller proudly writes, "My optimism . . . does not rest on the absence of evil, but on a glad belief in the preponderance of good and a willing effort always to cooperate with the good, that it may prevail."[13] The common element in the lives of all the world's most admirable people is that they are sustained by a passionate commitment to the happiness of others and to making a positive contribution to society. I am convinced that this noble spirit is the source of the robust optimism they exemplify in their lives for overcoming all difficulties.

MARINOFF: All people can make a significant difference for the better, especially when they align their positive energies with one another. Let me add that every human being can instantly be considered admirable whenever he or she makes any effort "to cooperate with the good." Dire problems confronting the world demand that we increase our supply of optimism in order that goodness may prevail. The noble spirit you identify as "the source of robust optimism" reminds me of what Lao Tzu asserted of Tao: that in use "it is inexhaustible."[14]

IKEDA: Toda said, "Once you are able to freely exercise the life force of the vast universe, you can stride boldly forward, completely unimpeded, in anything you do." In the Soka Gakkai

International, the goal of our faith is a daily life of continual self-improvement as we contribute to the well-being of others and of society as a whole. I want to progress together with young people, showing them that the spiritual world, the cosmos of life, is immeasurably vast and powerful.

Recovering Purpose and Connection

IKEDA: The advancement of modern science and technology is astounding. Progressing at a breathtaking pace, they are giving birth to one new development after another, materially enriching people's lives and increasing comfort and convenience. But people are again questioning whether these advances are actually enriching our spiritual lives or increasing our happiness.

MARINOFF: Used appropriately, technology has salutary effects on our social dimensions; used inappropriately, detrimental ones.

IKEDA: Technological progress is in essence a demonstration of human intellectual prowess. The critical issue is whether it is accompanied by the wisdom to use technology for human happiness.

The pros and cons of the Internet have been widely discussed. It has revolutionized communications, connecting people instantly around the world. On the other hand, the Internet has also given rise to many problems. It is used to harass people and violate their right to privacy and has become a breeding ground for new crimes against society.

In Japan as elsewhere, people are very concerned about children becoming addicted to violent video and online games and the deleterious effects those may have on personality development.

MARINOFF: In the United States, overindulgence in electronic media coupled with insufficient exposure to the written tradition has produced a generation with a great many socially dysfunctional and cognitively impaired children. Generally, Americans seem to worship death and violence on television—a culture of chronic necrophilia—yet are unprepared and unequipped to deal with death in personal and familial contexts.

IKEDA: The essential purpose of technology should be to contribute to human happiness. It is an unthinkable misfortune if technological advances are instead causing spiritual deterioration, severing social bonds, and isolating people from one another. More than a half-century ago, Dr. David Riesman, a leading twentieth-century sociologist, wrote in *The Lonely Crowd* of the social isolation and alienation characterizing American society.

MARINOFF: While its advantages and benefits are legion, you are quite correct to observe that technology has also weakened social and spiritual values in America. I recently met a husband and father of four children on a flight. He told me that the best thing that ever happened to his family was a prolonged power failure, during which family members congregated in one room and engaged in dialogue for the first time in years. Now they do it on a weekly basis.

SEVERED CONNECTIONS

IKEDA: That anecdote is indicative of the times. Many people today are pointing out the weakening of family ties and the loss of connections among human beings, between humans and nature, and between humans and their sense of eternity.

MARINOFF: In this context, three areas deserve special mention.

First, technologies have severed human connections to nature. Much like Emerson and Henry David Thoreau, you and I share a deep reverence for nature. Technocratic desecrations of and dissociations from nature have palpably weakened our sense of humanity.

Second, technologies have transposed much human interaction from real to virtual domains, making human bonds ephemeral instead of emotional. While email and cyberspace permit us to communicate across the global village independent of space and time, such interactions are only virtual, not real. As embodied beings, we need real human contact in order to experience our humanity. If not punctuated with episodes of reality, virtual interactions promote social dysfunction.

IKEDA: We are human beings, not machines. Human exchange— genuine communication through dialogue—is essential if we are to live fully human lives. Its absence can only lead to breakdown on both the individual and the larger social level.

MARINOFF: And we are witnessing such breakdowns.

Third, technologies have diverted people from being active producers to passive consumers. A hundred years ago, if family members wanted to hear music, they had to produce it themselves by learning instruments and playing either together or for one another. Producing music deepened their familial bonds. Nowadays, each family member is wired to his or her musical device, consuming his or her respective genres. The family dwells under the same roof but no longer shares the experience of producing music. Each family member is a node in a network instead of a member of a familial matrix.

IKEDA: Undeniably, families have fewer opportunities to create something together. Perhaps it is inevitable that as everything becomes more accessible, creative undertakings diminish. As you point out, people become mere consumers deprived of the satisfaction of shared achievement.

This may also have an adverse effect on our personal growth. After all, it is genuine communication and interaction among human beings that make us fully human. The eminent poet Rabindranath Tagore writes that "the human being loses sight of the self when existing in isolation; that is, the human being finds a larger and truer self in the context of many human relationships."[1] Only our interactions with others make our lives shine.

MARINOFF: Indeed, Tagore was both an outstanding poet and an exemplary humanitarian. It was he who gave Mohandas Gandhi the sobriquet *Mahatma*, meaning Great Soul.

The importance of familial and social relationships predates humans; they were a central feature of our primate evolution. As the pioneering primatologist Robert Yerkes wittily observed, "One chimpanzee is no chimpanzee."[2] And Aristotle writes, "He who is unable to live in society, or who has no need because he is sufficient for himself, must be either a beast or a god."[3] In light of this, the deconstruction of the family is surely at odds with our natural history.

CONFRONTING LIFE AND DEATH

IKEDA: Thank you for those compelling illustrations of a core truth. Speaking of families, I'm reminded of another recent social development related to the family. In the multigenerational families of the past, the most fundamental occurrences in life from beginning to end—birth, aging, illness, and death—were familiar events. But with advances in medicine, the loci of these events have shifted from the home to professional medical facilities. For 80 percent of Japanese, the final chapter of life takes place in hospitals or nursing homes. In other words, few people have opportunities to observe death as part of ordinary life. In contrast, it seems that in the West there's a growing trend to allow people to spend their last days at home.

MARINOFF: You make a significant point. If we fail to confront the issues of birth and death, which are the first and last pages of every life, then we may fail to read and write and understand the book of life itself. Technocracy has institutionalized both birth and death, robbing families of experiencing these precious beginnings and endings in natural ways. By consigning these events to hospitals, we over-medicalize their significance and undermine their vital human dimensions. In any case, those who do not confront birth and death are not fully alive.

IKEDA: Of course, the progress we've achieved in medicine over the centuries is one of humanity's golden achievements and has saved countless lives. There is the danger, however, that medicine may come to rely so heavily on technology that it reduces people to mere objects, devaluing them as living human beings. This is especially true at a time like now, when the medical field is becoming increasingly compartmentalized.

Life and death are fundamental philosophical issues. Buddhism takes as its starting point dealing with these supreme issues of life and death. Nichiren encourages us to "first of all learn about death, and then about other things."[4] Only by confronting the issues of life and death can we live in a more profound and meaningful way.

What's the true meaning of life and death? I believe this is the fundamental question facing modern civilization.

I touched on this in "Mahayana Buddhism and Twenty-first Century Civilization," my 1993 lecture at Harvard University:

We are beginning to understand that death is more than the absence of life; that death, together with active life, is necessary for the formation of a larger, more essential, whole. This greater whole reflects the deeper continuity of life and death that we experience as individuals and express as culture. A central challenge for the coming century will be to establish a culture based on an understanding of the relationship of life and death and of life's essential eternity.[5]

BEING FULLY PRESENT

MARINOFF: I am familiar with the contents of your Harvard lecture and find your views on the joy of life and the joy of death highly original. Although they may be accompanied by or indeed fraught with medical complications, birth, life, and death are neither completely captured nor exhaustively comprehended by medical technologies. The purpose of the medical arts and sciences is to help restore health and prevent illness, so that humans can have good births, lead good lives, and die good deaths.

IKEDA: Essentially, medicine must treat the whole human being—and physicians need to cultivate themselves as human beings, displaying an attitude of respect for the supreme worth and dignity of the life of each individual.

I have published a dialogue with Dr. Felix Unger, the president of the European Academy of Sciences and Arts and a celebrated cardiac surgeon who has operated on more than ten thousand patients (*Ningen shugi no hata o* [Hoisting the Banner of Humanism]). He described the ideal physician in this way: "We need doctors, not medical technicians. By doctor I mean a person whose personality is radiant in totality. A person who is warmly humane."[6]

The journalist Norman Cousins cited his concern over the growing number of physicians who "know more about disease than about people."[7]

MARINOFF: I share that concern. Empathy with humanity is indispensable to medical science because it is directly connected with human existence. As you know, I provide counsel to a range of clients: celebrities and CEOs, students and housewives, physicians and psychologists, young adults and retired persons. A journalist once asked me, "Who is your most interesting client?" I replied that my most interesting client is the next one to enter my office. Every person is important; every human problem requires resolution. In that sense, every case is notable.

IKEDA: The depth of your passion for humanity impresses me. You are always ready to open your heart and do your best for that "next client." Giving oneself wholly to the person in front of you—everything begins with this; it is the fundamental path of humanist philosophy.

MARINOFF: Thank you for emphasizing the importance of being fully present for others. The history of medicine has, of course, known outstanding humanitarians, from Hippocrates to Albert Schweitzer. Another was nurse Florence Nightingale, a pioneer of modern health care. Physician Norman Bethune saved thousands of lives performing surgery on battlefields in Spain and China, where he died of septicemia. And physician Albert Werckmann has devoted his life to nurturing and integrating autistic children into their local communities and economies.

So as you and Cousins assert, the proper education of doctors is not just a medical matter. I agree that it can and should extend to humanity, as currently exemplified by Doctors Without Borders.[8]

A GOOD LIFE, A GOOD DEATH

IKEDA: Some friends in the medical field once told me the story of a patient who, after successful surgery for cancer, suffered a recurrence and had to be hospitalized. About a week before he died, a nurse was checking on him. Although he was barely able to go to the bathroom by himself, he showed great concern for the other patients in the room, insisting to the nurse: "I am fine. Many other patients are waiting for you, so please attend to them first."

Knowing that the other patients were not in as serious a condition, the nurse was profoundly moved by his deep consideration. Soon, the patient died peacefully. In his final days, he evidenced a truly admirable state of being, in which he faced death without fear and remained filled with compassion for others.

I think we've all had the experience of trying to encourage someone and ending up being the one encouraged. Our true greatness, our happiness or unhappiness, is not determined by our objective circumstances. Being ill or having other problems does not necessarily mean that we are unhappy. The sick sometimes shine with a brilliant spirit, whereas the healthy may have nothing to show for their lives.

Toda used to observe that "people who have experienced grave illnesses are often full of life." He himself suffered from a serious illness, but even as he struggled with that, he continued his work for the sake of society and for peace. The key is to have a positive attitude and to live a fulfilled life, free from regrets, determined to overcome our difficulties.

MARINOFF: Many people take good health for granted, squandering the precious gift of life in pursuits that impoverish rather than enrich their life-condition. By contrast, the sustaining and enduring powers of humanity surely emanate from those who strive above all to lead a good life, however it may manifest. Does it not follow, then, that leading a good life and dying a good death are two sides of the same coin?

The patient to whom you refer died a good death, just as Socrates died a good death in ancient Athens. And given the inspiring life your mentor lived—so rich in vision for humanity, so blessed with success in your actualization of his vision—surely he must have died a good death, too, free of regret.

The poet William Blake writes, "Joy impregnates; sorrow brings forth."[9] Blake knew that one must taste suffering in order to bring forth that which is absolutely best within oneself. Is this not the kernel of Mahayana Buddhism?

OBSTRUCTIONS AS FUEL

IKEDA: A keenly perceptive, profound observation. In our dialogue, Toynbee says:

> Human dignity cannot be achieved in the field of technology, in which human beings are so expert. It can be achieved only in the field of ethics . . . . and ethical achievement is measured by the degree in which our actions are governed by compassion and love, not by greed and aggressiveness.[10]

Our ethical and spiritual development has not kept pace with the dramatic progress of science and technology. Toynbee earnestly sought ways to close the gap.

MARINOFF: The problem is how to overcome human greed and aggressiveness.

IKEDA: As I have mentioned, one key is to be found in the principle that earthly desires are the trigger for enlightenment, which is prominently articulated in the Lotus Sutra. Buddhism predating the Lotus Sutra taught that the obstructions of earthly desires that trouble our bodies and minds must be extinguished through long eons of practice in order for us to attain enlightenment. The Lotus Sutra, on the other hand, taught not how to eradicate those obstructions but how to convert them into the fuel for enlightenment. Toynbee was deeply impressed by this philosophy.

In Buddhism, the main obstructions to enlightenment are the "three poisons" of greed, anger, and foolishness, which destroy the roots of human goodness and plunge people into unhappiness. In modern terms, greed often takes the form of the endless pursuit of profit; anger is a manifestation of hurt and despair erupting as aggression and violence; and foolishness is the inability to recognize the dignity and worth of oneself and others. These poisons emerge from the ignorance that blinds us to the truth and leads to the destruction of both self and others.

Buddhism teaches that overcoming that ignorance is the path to resolving at the most fundamental level the sufferings of life and death. In other words, we need to redirect the energy manifested in selfish greed and anger toward universal prosperity and happiness, and convert the energy of foolishness to a life of service to others.

Nichiren Buddhism teaches the importance of an expansive, elevated life-condition. It reveals the concrete means to attain it, whereby we transform an existence shrouded in ignorance and delusion into one of wisdom, or enlightenment, transcending the sufferings of life and death. I believe this is an important perspective for both science and medicine to adopt.

MARINOFF: Buddhist teachings are always optimistic, offering constant promise for positive transformation. More and more Westerners, including health-care professionals, are becoming aware of this.

For example, I know a clinical psychologist who is a Chan Buddhist. He works with quite disturbed patients, people suffering from severe personality disorders. Such patients need a lot of care, and even then many of them cannot lead normal lives. But this psychologist has discovered that Chan Buddhist practices, such as sitting and chanting, act as a catalyst, making his patients much more responsive to all the other treatments. So Buddhism is medicinal, even in cases where poisons are abnormally deep-seated.

Western civilization has brought forth scientific technology, modern medicine, and material abundance. Medical technology has advanced to the point where it can micromanage the biology of life and death. But all of this is strikingly poor in terms of meaning and purpose.

My counsel to my clients may be summed up as encouragement to rediscover meaning in life. People can recover a sense of meaning and purpose by learning to recreate value for themselves and for others.

IKEDA: By discovering new meaning and creating new value, we can lead deeper and more consequential lives. This in turn will enable us to employ technology and all the other products of human ingenuity for the sake of happiness and social development. We stand in need of a sound philosophy that makes this possible. We need to restore our basic humanity as the starting point and measure for all things. Let's continue our dialogue for the sake of a philosophical renaissance to awaken the human race to such a new philosophy.

CONVERSATION SIX

All Are Worthy of Respect

IKEDA: The philosopher Martha Nussbaum, whom you quote in *The Big Questions*, offered this concise description of the essential role of philosophy: "The whole point of medical research is cure. So, too, the whole point of philosophy is human flourishing."[1]

In the Lotus Sutra, the Buddha says his land is one "where living beings enjoy themselves at ease."[2] On the strength of this passage, Toda always said that we are born into this world not to suffer but to enjoy ourselves. For people to lead enjoyable, vibrant, and meaningful lives in today's barren society, we need a philosophy that illuminates the individual mind like the light of the sun.

MARINOFF: Yes, an energizing, encouraging philosophy that maximizes the human potential to flourish is essential. Many factors or trends influence the current lack of such a philosophy. Let me sketch a couple of them here.

First, the great Quaker thinker Lewis Mumford identified one of the worst dangers as mass industrialization. He wrote that overexposure to machines and mechanistic lifestyles would induce a "mechanically engineered coma," in which people essentially somnambulate through life.³ Minds must be awakened in order to be illuminated. Cultures that numb awareness with television, video games, virtual realities, and designer drugs are putting people to sleep rather than waking them up to the dormant powers of their minds.

Second, twentieth-century Anglo-American philosophy itself has been dominated by the so-called analytic school, which views its mission as 100 percent theoretical and zero percent practical.

IKEDA: Of course, theory is important. But if philosophy fails to inspire or to resonate with people in the context of the challenges they face, all the theory and philosophy in the world are useless. Many people feel this way, I believe.

MARINOFF: This is precisely the issue with which I myself have grappled. The philosophies of people like Plato, Aristotle, Lao Tzu, Confucius, and others represent immortal human achievements. As I sought and practiced philosophies like theirs that reach the heart of human purpose, I became greatly interested in Buddhist thought and how it strengthens the inner person. Today, we are in great need of philosophies of this kind that encourage and heal.

IKEDA: Philosophy should be wisdom illuminating the meaning of life and awakening within us the power to live our lives well. It should encourage those who are suffering, helping them draw forth the inner strength they need to face life's challenges and hardships. This is what is so direly needed in today's society.

In *The Big Questions*, you give examples of practical philosophical counseling for children and students facing various problems, one of which is bullying. Perhaps conflict among children and even a bit of harmless fighting can be seen as a natural part of growing up, but bullying is something entirely different. Bullying is the insidious behavior of ganging up on certain students, ostracizing them, and subjecting them to mental pain and physical violence.

The fact that teachers and parents are often unaware that bullying is going on only increases the seriousness of the problem.

RESPONDING TO BULLYING

MARINOFF: Yes, bullying is a considerable problem in contemporary American and Japanese schools alike. One hears and reads about it continuously. My impression is that bullying has become a social epidemic. The responses, however—grounded in social work, psychology, and pharmacology—are symptomatic and clearly inadequate, since the problem only continues to worsen. We have a saying in the West, "An ounce of prevention is worth a pound of cure." Until and unless the root causes of bullying are identified and addressed, after-the-fact treatments are bound to be cosmetic and not curative.

IKEDA: I engaged in a dialogue about education for children with Albert A. Likhanov, an educator with many years' experience dealing with problems among Russian juveniles, which we published in book form (*Kodomo no sekai* [The Path to the Land of Children]).[4] He expressed deep concern over the rise in bullying as Russia has made rapid economic progress.

Bullying is obviously a problem in many countries. Many factors are involved, but it seems that both bullying and the general alienation that characterizes contemporary society can be traced back to a general inability to fully acknowledge the rights of others to exist and to afford them respect as fellow human beings. The failure to acknowledge and respect others is, in turn, inextricably linked to a lack of self-worth. They are, in fact, two sides of the same coin.

I'm reminded of a famous episode in the Buddhist scriptures, in which Shakyamuni is speaking to King Prasenajit and Queen Mallika of Kosala. No matter how they search, the Buddha tells them, people can never find anything more dear to them than their own self. This is equally true for each of us. Knowing how precious you are to yourself, he says, you must therefore never harm others.[5] Buddhism thus realizes that each person is of supreme importance to him- or herself. We must therefore refrain from harming others, for whom the self is equally precious.

This is a teaching of empathy, of caring for others as we care for ourselves. Surely, teaching and practicing this fundamental principle of human behavior at home and at school entail philosophy. A person who doesn't genuinely value him- or herself will find it hard to value others.

MARINOFF: What you say is of paramount importance. It seems clear that warmongers and mass murderers harbor enormous self-loathing rather than wholesome self-regard. Their failure to love themselves makes them capable of hating and annihilating others. This is bullying carried to its most vindictive and violent extreme.

As you suggest, cultivating in children ethics, moral self-worth, and regard for others is absolutely vital. Yet this fundamental duty has been neglected for decades, with appalling consequences.

I taught a master class in applied ethics for a group of CCNY's most gifted students, and they experienced a kind of revelation. In twenty years of formal education, not one of these students had ever been exposed to the ethics of Aristotle, Shakyamuni, or Confucius. They had been completely ignorant of the notion of virtue until they took this course. And these were the best students in the public system. This signals a catastrophic failure of American public education.

IKEDA: During their schooling, when they are building the foundation of their lives, young people should be exposed to a broad range of value systems and acquire the sound ethical grounding that we all need. And we, as adults, need to take the matters of values and ethics seriously ourselves.

Vincent Harding, a confidant of Martin Luther King Jr. in the nonviolence movement, once told me that many violent children believe they are important to no one. Events in the lives of juveniles undeniably mirror the pathologies, ethical failures, and corruption of the larger society. The root evil of contemporary society—that we have lost sight of the fundamental ethical principle that all people have value and are worthy of respect—is the deep undercurrent beneath many of the problems with which children and young people are suffering.

MARINOFF: This is the heart of the issue. In Tokyo, I have discussed with Soka educators and Soka schools counselors the problems encountered with bullying in public schools, which are, of course, outside the private Soka schools system. Apparently, some children are taunted and bullied for being "different," or individualistic, by intolerant coteries of conformists led by bullies. The same holds true in the United States. In Japan, it appears that many long-standing neo-Confucian norms—including those demanding humility and goodwill toward others—have been severely eroded by liberalization and globalization, thus weakening social constraints.

IKEDA: As many knowledgeable people point out, this diversification of values has altered traditional Japanese spirituality. Though people are searching for a sound philosophy of life and a fully human way of living, these are not easily found. I can't help thinking that, though our society is awash with material goods, the human spirit is being progressively impoverished, which creates a growing climate of desolation. Unfortunately, our children, society's greatest treasure, are the primary victims of this predicament.

MARINOFF: Of course, we must help children who suffer at the hands of bullies by encouraging them to feel morally worthy. But as you say, solely counseling the victims cannot redress the root cause of this problem: a social pathology. Offering psychological counseling to victims of bullying while failing to remedy the conduct of bullies themselves is analogous to offering palliative rather than preventive health care in cases where illness is avoidable.

IKEDA: Bullying is an absolute evil. Yet we often hear remarks to the effect that somehow the victim must also be to blame, which is nothing but a justification for the infliction of psychological and physical harm. The proper reaction to bullying is not to blame the victim but instead to speak out against the deep-seated lack of consideration for others demonstrated both by bullies and those who condone their behavior in any way. Adults must take a strong stand, declaring unequivocally that the blame lies with the bully, 100 percent. And, as you've said, we must strive to create an environment in which each child feels self-worth.

There's a definite decline in caring and consideration for others in modern society. This makes it all the more important for the family to be a place filled with love, providing warm and caring socialization. Unfortunately, in recent years, the family's capacity as a force for education and socialization has diminished significantly.

MARINOFF: Moreover, it appears that many children in Japan and elsewhere are not seeing enough of their fathers, who may commute and work long hours, leaving home before their children arise and returning after they go to bed. I believe that the problem of the so-called absent father contributes directly to bullying. Although not actually absent, fathers in these cases may fail to set healthy social models for their children.

IKEDA: When children grow up without learning in their families and schools how to behave and live together with other people—the basic norms of behavior and cooperation that all of us need to function in society—they often find themselves unnecessarily involved in conflict with others. This conflict can escalate into bullying.

In the past, various adults in the community played an informal, fatherly role in supervising, teaching, and socializing children, but recently the loss of community, especially in urban centers, has made this difficult. Children are losing the opportunity to learn even the most basic ethical principle—the difference between good and bad—that they formerly acquired through natural, informal interactions with adults in the community. As a consequence, many bullies are actually failing to recognize what they're doing as bullying.

MARINOFF: This vital point you're making is underscored in William Golding's cautionary novel *Lord of the Flies*, in which a group of so-called civilized English children are on a plane that crashes on a deserted tropical island. Bereft of adult authority and moral example, their civility swiftly evaporates. They degenerate into a savage mob, led by emergent bullies. Tragically, we are now witnessing the reenactment of Golding's allegory on a global scale.

Bullies are usually cowards. Courage in young males is best instilled by interaction with fathers and other mature males, who guide them through rites of passage into manhood and who also provide discipline when necessary.

This itself can become excessive to the extent of abuse. Abused boys may also become bullies, seeking to abuse others in turn. Many male juvenile delinquents have had either no father or an abusive one. Programs based on "tough love"[6] principles have provided a viable remedy. A stern but loving father figure disciplines these boys constructively, setting salutary goals for them and teaching them self-worth.

Maternal love, too, is necessary but by its nature is unconditional. Male children who receive only maternal love, without

complementary and conditional paternal love, may become infan-
tilized and not develop courage. While mothers adore their sons,
fathers set standards of manhood for them. The sons of absent or
abusive fathers are at risk for becoming bullies and need preventive attention. With daughters, the parental pattern is reversed:
fathers adore their daughters or sometimes, tragically, abuse them,
while mothers set standards of womanhood. But bullies are mostly
male children with absent or abusive fathers.

IKEDA: I see. What is ultimately behind bullying, whether we
speak of the collapse of moral standards or the decline of positive
male influences in child rearing, is the absence of sound moral,
ethical, and character values—"virtue" or "the good"—in adult
society. Children need the nurturing qualities that have traditionally been associated with both mothers and fathers, qualities that
are by no means restricted to actual mothers and fathers but can
be exercised by grandparents and many other adults involved in
children's lives. At one time, our schools and local communities
offered such support as well.

MARINOFF: Yes, adults are responsible for imparting correct standards of life to children. When adult society undervalues "virtue"
or "the good" and does nothing to correct its own discrimination
and fraud, it is unreasonable to demand morality from children.
The root causes of the problem remain unsevered.

In terms of bullying, children will only suffer more intensely as
long as community, home, and school do no more than prescribe
good behavior without addressing the core problems. Community,
home, and school are clearly interwoven, and each can offer solutions that recognize their interrelatedness. We must inculcate societal virtues, reinstate paternal leadership at home, and reintroduce
discipline in the schools.

IKEDA: As you say, cooperation and coordination among the three —society, home, and school—are key for the sake of children's happiness. Adults must take concrete steps and instill in children solid wisdom and bravery to overcome bullying.

When I spoke with her in the fall of 2006, Betty Williams, winner of the Nobel Peace Prize for her pacifist work in Northern Ireland, described how her granddaughter had been bullied at school. She advised the child to walk away, that nonviolence is the weapon of the strong. I feel certain these wise words were a great source of strength for the child.

In Asia, we have the expression "Adversity makes a man wise." Only by overcoming adversity and hardship do we polish and perfect ourselves. Never holding yourself back or limiting your potential—I think it's important for adults to offer children a model of this spirit of constant challenge and victory through our lives and actions.

MARINOFF: Eastern and Western philosophies converge on this point. Self-development depends on facing and surmounting challenges, while adversity has long been regarded as a way to draw upon the deepest resources of human character. As Lord Byron writes, "Adversity is the first path to truth."[7] Emerson teaches us how important it is to mobilize our inherent will power and limitless possibilities when he writes, "Adversity is the prosperity of the great."[8]

THE SUN WITHIN

IKEDA: In *The Big Questions*, you say that awakening is one of "Eight Ways Philosophy Can Change Your Life." This seems closely related to Buddhist philosophy. It is vitally important for human beings to awaken to their inherent possibilities and self-worth, not only because it cultivates self-confidence and courage but also because it fundamentally alters our attitudes toward other people. This is extremely important for all of us, not only children.

MARINOFF: Numerous life-changing insights of Western philosophy converge with Buddhism. This is especially true of the Platonic tradition, in which Emerson and his community of New England idealists were deeply immersed.

Surely, it is not by coincidence that a magnificent replica of Raphael's masterpiece *The School of Athens* adorns the stage at the Ikeda Auditorium of Soka University of Japan. I have visited the Ralph Waldo Emerson House in Concord, Massachusetts, where a sizeable replica of that very same painting hangs prominently over the mantel in his dining room.

Without a doubt, the Platonic tradition unwittingly reinvented key aspects of Buddhist philosophy, and it would be interesting to explore them in depth. For now, it is clear that you and I, perhaps like Emerson and Thoreau, both value Plato's tradition—precisely because it conceives of philosophy as a lifelong activity consecrated to illuminating the best qualities within every human being: by reflection, by dialogue, and by example.

IKEDA: In the Soka Gakkai International, we strive to shed light on and enhance the best qualities in all individuals by listening to their problems, offering encouragement, and sharing our sorrows and joys. Such encouragement is founded on courage and compassion. In Buddhism, compassion is defined as removing suffering and giving joy. While eliminating unhappiness and imparting peace of mind, the compassionate person joins with others to create and spread happiness.

The Japanese poet and author Toson Shimazaki writes that everyone can be the sun. Our responsibility is not to chase the sun in front of us, he says, but to raise high the sun within us. I believe the philosophical renaissance we have been talking about consists in allowing the sun, the power of life, within each individual to shine forth in full radiance. That's the light source for illuminating the future.

MARINOFF: Shimazaki's metaphor and your vision of a renaissance of philosophy are compelling indeed. They are also represented in Raphael's painting, whose central panel depicts, behind Plato and Aristotle, open archways leading to blue sky and bright sunlight. This is how Raphael understood the Italian Renaissance, which was based on neo-Platonism: philosophical inquiry leading to illumination. And as we know today, the very atoms of our bodies were forged by the sun, whose radiant light is also inherent in every human mind.

The Nature of Healing

IKEDA: The theme of healing is fundamental to philosophy, which has been called the balm of the human spirit. In *The Big Questions*, you start your "Eight Ways Philosophy Can Change Your Life" with a quotation on healing from the ancient Greek philosopher Epicurus:

> Vain is the word of a philosopher which does not heal any suffering of man. For just as there is no profit in medicine if it does not expel the diseases of the body, so there is no profit in philosophy either, if it does not expel the suffering of the mind.[1]

In this conversation, let's discuss healing—the nature of healing and the wounds that require it.

MARINOFF: I shall be pleased to discuss it with you. Healing is an important theme today because people are in great need of it.

IKEDA: In Japan, the word *healing (iyashi)* was heard far and wide in the 1990s, when an extended economic recession imposed hardships on many people. In fact, it became so much in vogue as to be named the national buzzword in 1999. The English verb *to heal* derives from the Old English *hal,* which conveys the meaning of "totality" or "completeness."

MARINOFF: Wholeness, wholesomeness, and integrity are indeed the original denotations of *hal.* To this day, we often describe healthy people in English as "hale and hearty."

IKEDA: The words *health* and *wholeness,* then, are related to healing.

MARINOFF: You cogently ground the deeper meaning of *health* in its Anglo-Saxon etymology. We can conceive of an integrated person as one whose various parts and aspects are aligned and functioning in concert, thus enabling optimal performance of one's being.

The Hellenic preoccupation with rational numbers reflected the Greeks' awareness of the importance of integral proportions. As you know, a rational number is one that can be represented as a ratio of two whole numbers (that is, integers). The Greeks perceived a connection between integral properties of numbers and human integrity. So they were upset at the discovery of irrational numbers (such as the square root of 2) because they feared that inherent irrationality in mathematics would doom ethics and politics to inherent irrationalities as well, making individual character flaws and collective political strife inevitable.

What is the etymology of *iyashi*? Does it bear a similar correspondence to wholeness and integrity?

IKEDA: The character used to write *iyashi* (癒) is rich with meaning. It's composed of two main elements, a radical meaning "illness" enclosing another element composed of two main parts: above, several ideographs that, taken together, depict lancing a boil with a large surgical knife; below, the character meaning "heart" or "mind." In other words, the character, taken as a whole, represents the idea of relieving illness and pain, restoring health, and bringing peace of mind.

Another interpretation is that the character's central part depicts a boat carved out of a log; the addition of "mind" below gives the character the meaning of carving out, or removing, ones worries. In this view, the two inner parts combined with the radical for "illness" give the meaning of carving out the illness from within our bodies.

These two explanations differ slightly in nuance, but they are alike in the sense that both mean "curing illness."

MARINOFF: In short, *iyashi* means to remove something bad and restore good health and wholeness.

LIFESTYLE MALADIES

IKEDA: This meaning of *iyashi* is very similar to the Buddhist concept of compassion, which comprises removing suffering and imparting joy. In general, *iyashi* is restoring both body and mind to the state of wholeness, a state of balance and harmony—in other words, health.

The World Health Organization defines *health* as a "state of complete physical, mental and social well-being and not merely the absence of disease or infirmity."[2] "Social well-being" refers to being engaged in a positive manner with one's environment, starting with the home and workplace.

Good health, then, is a state of balance and harmony in every aspect of your life. It is much more than the absence of sickness. This definition, however, is not universally accepted, it seems.

MARINOFF: The WHO definition is both true and somewhat idealistic, if not utopian. Even people of sound body and mind are implicated in social situations and conditions that are less than wholesome.

I have lived in the United States since 1994, and my general impression is that the American people's understanding of the meaning of *health* is increasingly poor. One is bound to conclude that the United States has become a chronically unwell society.

Can anyone be considered truly healthy in the complete sense, which seems tantamount to a kind of perfection not readily observable or attainable on this earth?

The current epidemic of obesity and overconsumption of junk food indicates little awareness of the nutritional dimension of good health. In tandem with this, far too many Americans exercise insufficiently or not at all, thus failing to take even the most rudimentary steps toward maintaining physical well-being.

IKEDA: Trends similar to those you describe as prevalent in the United States may be observed in Japan, too. To give just one example, about two-thirds of Japanese deaths are caused by what have come to be known as lifestyle maladies. As the name indicates, these are diseases caused by daily habits of diet, exercise, work, and rest. This is a widely recognized trend; the Germans call it *zivilisationskrankheit*, or "civilization diseases," and the Swedes *välfärdssjukdomar*, or "affluence diseases." Sadly, these illnesses are spreading rapidly among children, our treasures of the future.

MARINOFF: This is a really serious problem. The current Western epidemics—observable from Europe to North America—of obesity, bullying, hedonism, and consumerism, along with the decay of the social fabric, the deconstruction of education, the collapse of community, and the decline in birth rate, appear to be symptoms of a grievous and possibly terminal illness of Western civilization itself.

Insofar as Japan is Westernized, Japanese people suffer from it as well. An optimistic prognosis is that these widespread social disorders and cultural illnesses are in principle all reversible—a process that would depend on sound leadership, salutary example, effective education, inculcation of virtue, and alleviation of ignorance.

IKEDA: Though lifestyle maladies are not technically contagious, they can in a very real sense be passed from one person to another when people share the same lifestyle and environment. In July 2007, scholars at Harvard Medical School caused a great stir by announcing, after thirty-two years of research, that obesity can be passed to family members and friends.[3]

Children, naturally, are powerfully affected by their family environment. Acquiring sound health information and then practicing healthy living habits—important responsibilities that fall to adults—are indispensable for preventing lifestyle maladies. Each individual must learn to act wisely.

We also need to look critically at the direction in which our society is moving and change it if necessary. Critically examining information and customs is another important role for philosophy to play, isn't it?

MARINOFF: Yes, it is. Philosophy teaches critical thinking skills that are invaluable in everyday life and essential for professionals of every kind. In terms of critically examining norms and customs, philosophers play the Nietzschean role of physicians to culture.

Assessing the United States in this light, we can see that its intellectual capital is in precipitous decline. The education system has been purged of content, while the media pander incessantly to the demand for celebrity scandal and callow sensationalism. Overexposure to visual media coupled with institutionalized inattention to the written tradition have produced a generation of cognitively impaired children, millions of whom are daily drugged with stimulants.

Notwithstanding all this, many Americans still seem to believe that money will solve all their problems. In fact, I have never seen so much unhappiness amid such affluence.

IKEDA: In certain respects, it's increasingly difficult to live a healthy life today. It's a struggle. We need to "win" our health through intelligence and effort.

And for some people, the experience of illness can trigger a deeper view of life and its purpose, leading to a more worthwhile life. I know many people making a positive contribution to the health of society, even though they may not be perfectly healthy themselves.

By the same token, freedom from physical illness does not necessarily mean one is living a fulfilling and healthy life. As the Buddhist scriptures put it, "Though someone may have great physical strength, if he lacks a resolute spirit, even his many abilities will be of no use."[4] This is why it's important for us to think deeply about what constitutes a truly healthy life.

THE MIND RULES THE BODY

MARINOFF: Perhaps true good health consists in our ability to maintain serenity and manifest beneficence, even when obliged to endure afflictions of various kinds, be they medical, emotional, or social. As an example, consider Casals.

IKEDA: Casals, whom we've already mentioned in our discussion of the importance of praise and encouragement (see Conversation Three), lived a long life devoted to peace.

MARINOFF: He once injured his hand in a climbing accident, obliging him to cancel months of concerts and undergo lengthy rehabilitation. People expected him to be demoralized, if not depressed. Instead, he was beaming with joy. His first thought, he later reported, was, "Thank God, I'll never have to play the cello again!"[5] I believe this is an example of true good health—a condition in which one's serenity remains unaffected by injury.

Ideally, such serenity would be undiminished even in the face of catastrophic loss or impending death. So perhaps true good health consists in one's ability to, in the Buddhist sense, "make good causes" in any set of circumstances, no matter how dire.

IKEDA: This is indeed essential in life. As you make clear, the mind is the important thing. In Buddhist terms, "the mind is the ruler of the body."[6] In a time of anxiety and stress—in the state you have termed not "disease" but "dis-ease"—the ability to summon up a positive attitude is crucial. The all-too-frequent tendency is to try to run away from such situations or to become passive and let them overwhelm us. Even if we discover some temporary method of relieving the anxiety or stress we're facing, it's often not a true solution; when we find ourselves in similar circumstances again, we'll experience the same anxiety and stress.

Consequently, as you say, it's necessary to "make good causes" in any situation, however trying. Who is it that must do this? Each of us, ourselves. We need to tap the strength that is inherently ours, the inner potential that is ours, the power of life that is ours. To me, this is where, in any age—but more so in our present time than any other—philosophy and religion come into play in a major way.

MARINOFF: Yes, they do. I should like to include one further factor in our exploration of true good health: emancipation, which is one of the eight effects of philosophy I discuss in *The Big Questions*. As I mentioned (see Conversation One), I cite your related words: "Life is filled with truly unfathomable potential . . . in most cases, our so-called limitations are nothing more than our own decision to limit ourselves."[7] The implications of this statement are profound. It suggests that true good health must take into account not only infirmity and incapacity, injury and injustice, but also the extent to which a return to optimal functionality or vital being requires the removal of self-imposed impediments.

IKEDA: Yes, we must not give up on ourselves. What we need more than anything in times like ours is the "can do!" energy of hope. Buddhism teaches that the greatest joy comes from awareness that the noblest, worthiest possible life-condition exists right here within our own hearts and minds, and that failing to be aware of this supreme inner worth is ignorance.

MARINOFF: I am acquainted with many people who are unhealthy because they are unhappy, are unhappy because they are unfulfilled, and are unfulfilled because they themselves have obstructed their fulfillment.

For example, one of my clients was a professional woman who earned much money on Wall Street but suffered from hypertension. Her husband had a parallel profession in a high-pressure Manhattan law firm. Although free of material worries, both she and her husband were in permanent states of stress and unhappiness.

Via philosophical counseling, this woman found a spark of encouragement to remove their obstructions. She and her husband now operate a gardening and landscaping business in a rural community. They are happy and fulfilled, even though they earn less money. More important, their work serves to beautify people's homes and environments, and so their own lives are daily infused with beauty.

THE NOTION OF VITALISM

IKEDA: Nichiren uses the following metaphor to express the effects of altruism: "If one lights a fire for others, one will brighten one's own way."[8]

The couple you describe chose a way of life that rejoiced in the happiness of others, earning them the gratitude of people in their community. It's not the details of the specific work in this anecdote that matter, since all of us have unique talents and are suited for different occupations. What's crucial here is the couple's determination to change their environment, which reflects considerable personal growth.

Hope springs from personal change, from self-transformation at the deepest level of being. We all have our failings, of course, large or small. What we need to do is wisely and with a positive attitude try to clear them away and draw forth a new creativity from within. The educational philosopher John Dewey believed that humanity has an "undiscovered resource"—human beings themselves.[9]

We all possess unlimited inner potential. It seems to me that the way to lead a truly healthy life is to develop one's unique potential to the fullest and at the same time create value for others and society.

MARINOFF: To couch wellness or health in terms of vitality is to open a philosophically interesting avenue: namely, the notion of vitalism itself. The idea that life embodies a vital force has been discredited but hardly disproved by twentieth-century advances in materialistic biology. If the nature of healing is that which restores vitality, then we must allow for the existence of a vital force that uniquely animates living beings.

IKEDA: What is life? This is the fundamental question facing humanity. Nichiren Buddhism defines life's highest attributes in terms of the three meanings of *myo* (the mystic or wondrous): "to open," "to be fully endowed," and "to revive." "To open" means unfolding the limitless possibilities of life. "To be fully endowed" refers to the unifying and integrating function of life, harmonizing all things through wisdom and compassion. "To revive" means restoring what has been damaged or lost and enabling those things to manifest their strengths. Releasing these energies located in the depths of our beings provides the source of power we need to lead creative lives.

Buddhism also teaches that the individual is a microcosm, likening the roundness of the human head to the heavenly sphere, the hair to the stars, the eyebrows to the seven constellations of the northern hemisphere, the eyes to the sun and the moon, and the opening and closing of the eyes to day and night. Nichiren posits that the "sun, moon, and myriad stars are found in one's life,"[10] offering a truly grand, expansive view of life.

In other words, the rising sun, the serene pure light of the moon, and the sparkling of the stars in the heavens are all to be found within our own beings. No matter how dark the times in which we live, we are shining suns. We embody the wondrous Law permeating the entire universe. A time of healing is an opportunity to regain the well-balanced, healthy state that our lives originally possess.

MARINOFF: Most people try to sustain a balance of well-being, which may amount to an equilibrium of vital being. This equilibrium can be unbalanced by internal and/or external perturbations that give rise to unhappiness or unwellness. Healing, then, is any intervention or process that enables or causes the restoration of vital being.

Healing the Wounds of Arbitrary Division

IKEDA: Life is so immediate and familiar to us as to seem commonplace on the one hand, yet it is a profound wonder and mystery on the other. On the wondrousness of life, Tagore says, "Human beings can rely on their own power only if they realize that the universal law is inherent in themselves."[1]

In our previous conversation, we discussed healing as a restoration of the wholeness of life and how to tap the inner life force that is the key to that restoration. How does life operate, how does it work? How can we enhance its power? These are very important yet difficult questions. As a preface to considering these, I'd like to present a simple explanation of the Buddhist doctrine of the ten life-conditions, also known as the Ten Worlds.

MARINOFF: Please do so. I was happy to encounter a lucid exposition of the Ten Worlds, geared to a British readership, in the excellent book *The Buddha in Daily Life* by the late Richard Causton, first general director of the Soka Gakkai International in the United Kingdom. I adapted his version for an American readership in *The Big Questions*.

IKEDA: Mr. Causton, always the English gentleman, was an unforgettable friend and treasured comrade.

The Ten Worlds theory derived from the Lotus Sutra is the basis for the teaching of three thousand realms in a single moment of life,[2] formulated by Zhiyi. He categorized human life based on its dominant characteristics into ten realms or worlds, ranging from hell to Buddhahood. From instant to instant, these states are manifested, triggered by various contributory causes.

The Ten Worlds are as follows:

(1) The world of hell, a state of being constrained by suffering;

(2) The world of hunger, in which one suffers from the inability to attain one's desires;

(3) The world of animality, in which one fears the strong but despises those weaker than oneself;

(4) The world of anger, in which one looks down on others and seeks to dominate them;

(5) The world of humanity, in which one preserves a stable frame of mind and judges things calmly;

(6) The world of heaven, in which one is filled with the joy of having realized one's desires;

(7) The world of learning, in which one has awakened to impermanence through hearing the Buddhist teachings;

(8) The world of realization, in which one attains partial enlightenment on one's own through apprehending the laws governing natural and other phenomena;

(9) The world of bodhisattva, in which one strives for one's own enlightenment while, at the same time, taking action to communicate and spread the teachings of Buddhism to benefit others;

(10) The world of Buddha, or Buddhahood, the most powerful, enjoyable, and correct way of life possible. In this condition, life reaches its epitome, and one can freely exercise the powers of fortitude, wisdom, and compassion.

Buddhism teaches that life is ceaselessly and dynamically shifting and changing. As Nichiren puts it, "A single person in the course of a single day has eight million four thousand thoughts."[3] Some may, within a single day, move back and forth among the worlds of hell, hunger, and animality (the so-called three evil paths, or, with the inclusion of anger, the four evil paths), experiencing a low, barbarous life-condition. Others may remain for a long time in the world of bodhisattva. And the length of these experiences of suffering or fulfillment will also differ from person to person.

The Buddha world—the Buddha state of life—is not anomalous or remote from our lives. It exists fully in and from the beginning of everyone's life. The purpose of Buddhist teachings and practice is to enable us to manifest it.

How have American readers responded to this Buddhist view of life described in your book, and what do you think of it?

MARINOFF: Thank you for this elegant synopsis of the ten life-conditions, which certainly helps me understand them better. A good many of my readers, internationally, have responded very positively to Buddhism or at least to my philosophical version of it. I have had occasions to teach the Ten Worlds at The City College of New York, where students hail from 150 countries.

Allow me to share something special with you that occurred after a recent course I gave on Buddhism. As you know, a growing number of Jews and Christians have embraced Buddhist philosophy and practice. But Buddhism has not yet penetrated as broadly into the Islamic branch of these Abrahamic faiths. Nevertheless, one of my Muslim students sent me the following unsolicited testimonial:

> Buddhism has had a profound effect on me since I started learning about it in Buddhism class. Even though I was born and raised as a Muslim and plan on staying a Muslim for the rest of my life, a lot of the things that were discussed

> in class related and resonated with me. The philosophy of
> Buddhism is what related to me.

Clearly, Buddhism's humanistic philosophy has reinforced the noblest aspects of his faith. This augurs well for Buddhism's propagation through Islamic cultures, even if that requires decades or centuries.

As for mainstream American culture, its audiences have minimal interest in philosophy. America is an incarnation of ancient Rome, not of ancient Greece; Americans are habituated to circuses, not concepts. American culture is so psychologized and over-medicated that Freudian models and mood-enhancing medicines govern its life-condition. With what result? Americans over-populate the lowest four realms of the Ten Worlds.

Thus, I am sure that many Americans would welcome the emancipating insight of the Ten Worlds, if only there were more opportunities to make them aware of it.

THE FIRST CONDITION OF HEALING

IKEDA: I understand. The significance of your pioneering ideas will no doubt gain greater appreciation with the passage of time.

One of the important points of the teaching of the Ten Worlds is that it offers a concrete explication of the phenomena of happiness and unhappiness based on our innermost beings. The Lotus Sutra teaches that each of the Ten Worlds possesses the potential for all ten within itself, a doctrine called the mutual possession of the Ten Worlds. This means that the state of Buddhahood exists within the life of each individual right now, at the present moment. But it may be obscured by ignorance.

The teachings of Buddhism are aimed at enabling us to transform whatever situation we are in. In other words, the power of healing exists within each of us from the very beginning.

MARINOFF: I sympathize with the Buddhist view. The first condition of healing is surely awareness. People must become aware that to be alive in sentient human form presents an unparalleled opportunity to mobilize the enormous potential of their life force. Their healing powers can be restored only when they understand that such resources lie within them and that their health need not be passively dependent upon external powers.

IKEDA: Yes, that's the crux of the problem. The teachings of Nichiren Buddhism describe "the great joy that one experiences when one understands for the first time that one's mind from the very beginning has been a Buddha."[4] When you awaken to the tremendous worth and dignity of your life, you're able to tap inexhaustible healing power. Each of us is the greatest of all healers.

The next issue is, precisely what are we healing? It's crucial to accurately identify our wounds that need healing.

MARINOFF: Perennial wounds stemming from attachments, desires, mental poisons (such as anger, greed, and envy), and ignorance of the true causes of suffering must be healed in every generation.

IKEDA: In terms of the doctrine of the Ten Worlds, the realms of hell, hunger, animality, and anger cause those wounds. The focus in Buddhism is on elevating our life-condition, lifting it from the narrow egotism exemplified by those realms to the progressively more expansive, open realms of learning, realization, the bodhisattva, and the Buddha. The main point of the theory of the Ten Worlds is to carry out our human revolution and transform a petty, narrow, self-centered self into the greater self, seeking the happiness of self and others alike.

In Buddhist thought, as I mentioned earlier (see Conversation Five), narrow egotism is a manifestation of the three poisons—

greed, anger, and foolishness—the obstructions to enlightenment that underlay our sense of self. Such egotism is the obstruction that causes unhappiness in our lives.

Nichiren observes that "famine occurs as a result of greed, pestilence as a result of foolishness, and warfare as a result of anger."[5] In other words, the stronger the activity of the three poisons, the more they compromise our health, destroy our mental and physical balance, and bring turmoil to society at large.

COMMUNITY WOUNDS

MARINOFF: We need to consider the subsequent wounds to be healed for society as a whole. Every human community—whether familial or tribal, religious or national—has its particular wounds that require healing. But if we speak of society as a whole, meaning the single human community that inhabits our global village, then the wounds that most urgently need healing are precisely those that divide this global society into mutually antagonistic parts.

IKEDA: We all are members of the human race and share the destiny of the global community. During the height of the Cold War, Toda was one of the first to discuss global citizenship, in which all human beings, transcending national and ethnic differences, are fellow citizens of one planet. Acutely perceiving the evils that divide human beings, he sounded a warning against the social pathology of elevating ideological and nationalistic considerations over those of human life as a whole.

MARINOFF: You were fortunate to have had such a visionary mentor as Toda. Millions of Soka Gakkai International members now share in that good fortune since you, having understood and acted on his warning, have given precedence to human dignity over baser considerations. Yet even though the Cold War is over, millions of people continue to be embroiled in divisive ideological conflicts.

IKEDA: Unless we correct the mistaken ideologies and prejudiced views behind conflict and schism, there can be no essential cure for society's wounds.

MARINOFF: In other words, society as a whole suffers from wounds that cause it to regard itself as less than whole. Only when human society regards itself as whole will its divisive wounds be healed.

IKEDA: A very important point. In commenting on examples of the loss of humanity that accompany technological advances in modern society, you have cited Emerson: "The reason why the world lacks unity, and lies broken and in heaps, is because man is disunited with himself."[6] This disunity, I presume, is the failure to manifest the wholeness and fully integrated nature of life. In this disunited condition, our lives are fundamentally warped, damaged, and discordant.

MARINOFF: Sadly, this is so. Emerson was extraordinarily prescient in his understanding of the dehumanizing effects of advancing technology. At the inception of the scientific and industrial revolutions, optimists saw opportunities for emancipating human beings from hard labor and daily drudgery, thereby enhancing their quality of life immeasurably. But the excesses of the Industrial Revolution ended up mechanizing humanity itself, just as excesses of cybernetic technologies are currently virtualizing people, further divorcing them from reality.

The disunity of which Emerson writes is indeed more palpable today and can be remedied only by a return to wholeness. For Emerson and his community of New England idealists, this was most readily accomplished by communing regularly with nature, as Thoreau did.

TO BE TRULY HUMAN

IKEDA: Their community was the philosophical galaxy of the nineteenth-century American Renaissance. I've been an avid reader of Thoreau's *Walden* since my youth. That's why I feel so privileged to have published a dialogue with Dr. Ronald A. Bosco and Dr. Joel Myerson, both past presidents of the Thoreau Society, on the philosophy of the American Renaissance (*Creating Waldens*, 2009).

Emerson urges that human beings return to nature in order to live creatively and true to their highest potential:

> As I walked in the woods . . . and uplifted into the infinite space, I became happy in my universal relations. . . . The whole of nature addresses itself to the whole man. We are reassured. It is more than a medicine. It is health.[7]

Emerson's philosophy, which incorporated much Asian thought, is still shedding light on the whole world today. Thoreau, who responded to Emerson and put his ideas into practice, warned that, in a society devoted to the pursuit of wealth and convenience, "men have become the tool of their tools."[8] When he said this, the English Industrial Revolution was reaching America.

MARINOFF: And now, a century and a half later, modernity and its challenger, postmodernism, both waylay humanity's quest for sustainable happiness.

In late August 2001, I spent an idyllic summer day in Concord, walking Emerson's and Thoreau's former pathways, communing with their great spirits. That day touched me to the core of my being. Its lingering serenity was soon shattered by the events of September 11, 2001, yet the twin towers of Emerson's and Thoreau's idealism continue to stand tall, unscathed by human conflagration.

As you surmise, Asian thought certainly influenced Emerson. His protégé Thoreau's philosophy of nonviolent civil disobedience meanwhile came to exert seminal influence on Tolstoy, Gandhi, King, and yourself. The New England idealists were both reflectors and transmitters of perennial wisdom—of ideas that heal all humankind.

As long as humans spend most of their waking hours emulating cogs in machines or nodes in networks, the disintegration of self and society—as well as the planetary despoliations that such disintegration spawns—will only worsen.

IKEDA: I share your concern. To reiterate an earlier point (see Conversation Five), people today are losing wholeness because of the rupture of three kinds of relationships—that of individual and society, human beings and nature, and body and spirit. Our times can only be described as ailing. Society itself is indeed in need of healing.

Our bodies and minds are originally one. Buddhism articulates this as the essential oneness of body and mind. Another Buddhist doctrine, the oneness of life and its environment, elucidates the essential oneness and inseparability of the living being and its environment. Buddhism sees the individual as a microcosm corresponding to the macrocosm of the universe, as I have said earlier (see Conversation Seven). In addition, from the perspective of Buddhism, the individual, human society, nature, the earth, and the entire universe constitute one great life entity.

Buddhism also teaches that a single thought of the microcosm, the human individual, encompasses the great life entity of the entire universe. I am firmly convinced that, from the viewpoint of healing as the restoration of wholeness, the Buddhist concept of life is very important.

MARINOFF: The unities you outline are insightful and pertinent. Lost in multiplicity, Westerners often lose sight of the one. By contrast, as you have said, those who experience wholeness in themselves exert similar influences upon their environments.

A "HEALTHY EGO"?

IKEDA: As the first step in your practical philosophy, you stress the importance of recognizing one's current state. You emphasize the need to start by asking if one's present condition is one of disease or its psychological corollary, dis-ease. This is crucial advice.

In terms of the Ten Worlds, the condition of dis-ease corresponds to the three evil paths or the four evil paths. Disease demands medical treatment, but in overcoming suffering, or dis-ease, the self is always the active agent.

The question then becomes, how does one acquire a deep understanding of one's present condition, how does one see it for what it actually is? This is an important step in self-transformation. But the fact is that it's very hard, I believe, to really know one's true state.

MARINOFF: Yes, it can be difficult indeed. A lamp illuminates its surroundings, not its inner workings. The self cannot truly know itself, yet it can deceive itself. The egoistic, self-deceived self forges fetters to dis-ease, while ease emanates bountifully from the non-self. The truly vital transformation is therefore from self to non-self.

But this can take a long time to realize. While it is healthy to seek to transform dis-ease into ease, attempting to do so by direct appeals to the self are bound to create only more dis-ease.

I firmly believe that the notion of a "healthy ego" is an oxymoron. By definition, the ego is unhealthy and the very source of dis-ease.

My advice to people undertaking such a search is to solicit as many trustworthy opinions as possible, whether from family, friends, or professional helpers of various kinds. Beyond this, one can consult a wealth of books on philosophy and psychology, Eastern and Western alike. One should never become discouraged or confused when professional opinions diverge or contradict one another, for the approach to truth is not necessarily a simple or straightforward path. As Cicero in ancient Rome and John Stuart Mill in Victorian England both knew, truth often emerges from contending positions or adversarial debates.

The important thing is to make a sincere effort to "know thyself" and make progress toward "knowing thy non-self." Dis-ease must ultimately be traced to, and expunged from, its roots.

IKEDA: What should family or friends offering counsel keep in mind in trying to help the person determine his or her present state?

MARINOFF: The attitude of no attitude would be best, although it is difficult to practice with those closest to us. I can best assist my clients by listening to them and by trying to understand their situations, rather than by imposing my beliefs or prejudices on them. The same is even truer with family and friends.

WE ARE ALL HEALERS

IKEDA: The ancient Greek philosopher Zenon says, "This is why we have two ears and only one mouth, that we may hear more and speak less."[9] We must make a genuine effort to listen to others.

MARINOFF: A succinct metaphor. Familiarity and closeness can invite habitual or subjective judgments instead of objective assessments. To be truly helpful, one must consider the condition of the other from a standpoint of beneficent advocacy and selfless impartiality. This can often be achieved more easily with strangers or friends than with family.

IKEDA: The same supportive attitude can be a source of strength in the medical treatment of patients. I met twenty years ago with Nobel Peace Prize laureate Bernard Lown, the cofounder of the International Physicians for the Prevention of Nuclear War. He lamented the loss of a focus on healing, as opposed to mere treatment, in modern medical practice. As therapeutic technology advances, he noted, the number of doctors willing to listen to what patients have to say has diminished. The dialogue between physicians and their patients that is so critical to tapping the patients' self-healing powers has disappeared. The loss of a focus on healing, he argued, is directly linked to the absence of dialogue—a position that completely agrees with your own.

MARINOFF: Unfortunately, you and Dr. Lown are correct. Great scientific and technological advances in medicine notwithstanding, the industry of health care increasingly treats illnesses and not persons. The process is dehumanizing for all concerned: doctors, allied caregivers, and patients alike. The family doctor, or personal physician, is a relic of the past, replaced by impersonal technocracy.

IKEDA: This is a big problem. It's why patients who encounter good doctors are fortunate.

As Lown said in an interview for the *Seikyo Shimbun*, the Soka Gakkai's daily newspaper, physicians must rethink their role as not only curing their patients' bodies but also healing their minds, their spirits. A doctor who cannot heal is a doctor who has forgotten the art of listening to patients, he added, and proper listening starts with respect for the speaker.

Healing begins with respect for the other party and the willingness to listen, and these ingredients apply to more than the doctor-patient relationship. In an age when disregard for others is so widespread, this is a principle that each of us should strive to practice.

MARINOFF: Each individual must accept the responsibility of a healer in his or her own way. The bodhisattva spirit can be realized by anyone in any profession. This is the quintessence of the teaching of the Ten Worlds. Only when each person accepts the responsibility of healing can dis-ease be reduced to an insignificant level.

CONVERSATION NINE

The Healing Power of Dialogue

IKEDA: You live in Monroe, Orange County, in the countryside north of New York City.

MARINOFF: Yes, I do.

IKEDA: Coincidentally, Soka University of America, which I founded, is located in another Orange County, in California. So "Orange County" has a special ring to me.

MARINOFF: I'm glad it does. That's an interesting connection. I have visited the university and found it a wonderful place—its architecture and landscaping are beautiful. These two Orange counties, one on either coast, are like geographic bookends to the United States.

IKEDA: I understand that, with its forests and lakes, Monroe has a beautiful natural setting.

MARINOFF: Yes, it does. Nearby is Harriman State Park, with sixty thousand acres of pristine woods and lakes. And the famed

Appalachian Trail cuts right through Monroe itself. I hope you will visit someday.

Ikeda: Thank you. I would like to very much.

Marinoff: The town was named for James Monroe, the fifth US president. Blessed with natural resources of lime and iron, the region had been a center of iron mining since the eighteenth century. In addition, the first cheesery in America was established in Monroe, whose original name (in 1799) was Cheesecock.

Ikeda: That's very interesting from a historical viewpoint. How do you travel to New York City?

Marinoff: I always commute by bus and subway from Monroe to the campus of The City College of New York.

Ikeda: I would like to visit the campus, too.

Marinoff: By all means. We would be honored by your visit.

Ikeda: I actually have a connection with The City University of New York (the public university system to which City College belongs). In January 2000, Queens College conferred on me an Honorary Doctorate in Humane Letters.

Marinoff: Yes, among hundreds of your well-deserved honors. And here is another interesting connection: Dr. Allen Sessoms, president of Queens College at that time and current president of the University of the District of Columbia (since September 2008), is also my friend. He admires you greatly.

Ikeda: I am honored. Please extend my best wishes to Dr. Sessoms.

To change the subject somewhat, I understand that the US floral emblem, or national flower, is the rose.

MARINOFF: Yes.

IKEDA: I understand it is the official flower of New York State, too.

MARINOFF: Yes. The Cranford Rose Garden of the Brooklyn Botanic Garden, one of the most celebrated of its kind in the country, has more than 5,000 rose plants of 1,400 varieties.

IKEDA: It is one of the famous sights of the city. Long a favorite in Japan, the rose appears in the eighth-century poetry anthology the *Man'yoshu* (Collection of Ten Thousand Leaves) and is mentioned in *The Tale of Genji*, written a millennium ago. As the name suggests, the variety known as *Rosa Chinensis* came to Japan from China.

MARINOFF: You rounded out your 1991 Harvard lecture with a famous quotation from Emerson, in which he praises the beauty of the rose and of friendship:

> O friend, my bosom said,
> Through thee alone the sky is arched,
> Through thee the rose is red,
> All things through thee take nobler form
> And look beyond the earth,
> The millround of our fate appears
> A sunpath in thy worth.
> Me too thy nobleness has taught
> To master my despair;
> The fountains of my hidden life
> Are through thy friendship fair.[1]

IKEDA: I remember well the occasion of that lecture. Titled "The Age of Soft Power," my lecture spoke of the need to revive a philosophy that can elevate the level of our humanity. That's why I'm so happy to have this opportunity to befriend you and engage in a deeply meaningful discussion with a great philosopher of your caliber. I hope that this dialogue will spiritually nourish as many of our readers as possible, enriching their lives and contributing to their good health.

MARINOFF: You are most generous. In turn, I must say that engaging in this dialogue with you is a life-altering privilege for me—a unique opportunity to philosophize with the most accomplished Buddhist leader of our age. Inspired by your example, I join my hope to yours: that our words will create value for all who chance to read them. To that end, shall we return to our current question concerning dialogue's healing power?

DIALOGUE BASED ON MUTUAL TRUST

IKEDA: Felix Unger emphasizes that compassion is the foundation of all healing. It is a source of incomparable strength for all of us. He also writes that compassion is manifested in the most ordinary forms of behavior, such as offering warm words of encouragement or being a good, caring listener. When would you say people find their personal relations healing and restorative?

MARINOFF: In cases of dis-ease, people have the capacity to heal themselves but often require dialogue to activate that capacity. In other words, we must co-create a reflective space in which people are heard, understood, and valued but not judged. That is when personal relations are their most restorative. Only then are people free to fathom the depths of their dis-ease to its bottom. At that moment, their healing powers will begin to function maximally.

For example, I recall counseling a young woman in Palermo,

Italy, in a demonstration session for Sicilian philosophical counselors. This posed special challenges, as it was conducted via an interpreter in front of a camera and an audience. The young woman was self-obstructed, unable to grant herself permission to pursue a path of fulfillment. In consequence, she was trapped in unhappiness.

After about thirty minutes of dialogue, she suddenly achieved a breakthrough and understood that she held the keys to her liberation. Afterward, when asked what had prompted her breakthrough, she said it was the counselor's "kind eyes." She taught me a great lesson concerning the power of kindness to catalyze healing.

IKEDA: What a splendid story. You interacted with this woman as a fellow human being, not just as a counselor. In your dialogue, you really listened to her problems, meeting her as an equal instead of placing yourself at some higher, "professional" distance. That must be why she responded to your genuine wish to relieve her suffering. Your approach then drew out her own capacity for healing and enabled her to make that crucial breakthrough.

The eyes are very powerful. In fact, a compassionate gaze is considered a form of giving in Buddhism.

Acknowledging and sympathizing with another's pain through such a dialogue based on mutual trust—the communication process shared between two individuals in order to open that "reflective space" you speak of—is the starting point for healing. What is most important for attaining this kind of a genuine meeting of the minds in dialogue?

MARINOFF: We should relate to other people as human equals. We should engage them in dialogue as inquirers, seeking to learn about their dis-ease, aspiring to understand but not to judge them, instilling in them the confidence to remedy and not to wrong themselves, valuing and appealing to their most salutary inner qualities.

Any dialogue conducted on this basis will almost certainly be helpful and not harmful to all parties. In such a dialogue, we should eschew the hierarchical nature of relationships based on social standings or professional positions.

IKEDA: I agree. The bodhisattva named Never Disparaging, who appears in the Lotus Sutra, greets everyone he meets by bowing reverently and saying:

> I have profound reverence for you, I would never dare treat you with disparagement or arrogance. Why? Because you are all practicing the bodhisattva way and will then be able to attain Buddhahood.[2]

This profound respect for others is the essence of Buddhism.

There are few opportunities for meaningful dialogue with others in today's fast-paced, disconnected society. Instead of enjoying genuine communication, many are suffering in isolation.

That's why it's so important to put aside our differences and really listen to others, sharing their pains and sufferings as fellow human beings. The caring heart capable of listening in this way has the power to open people's minds, to dispel anxiety, and to heal mental wounds. It takes a human heart to touch a human heart.

"When you're suffering, I hurt, too." By engaging in dialogue in this spirit of empathy—what is called in Buddhism "shared suffering"—both parties are strengthened and elevated.

A THERAPEUTIC ALLIANCE

MARINOFF: A growing number of philosophical counselors, as well as psychological and medical counselors, are becoming aware of the efficacy of Buddhist approaches to dialogue.

Speaking from experience as a philosophical practitioner, I

would say that dialogue is of paramount importance in facilitating the healing of dis-ease, whether in personal, professional, or organizational life. All reputable counselors know that the key to healing their clients consists in establishing with them a therapeutic alliance, which is achieved through dialogue.

IKEDA: What you're describing is the creation of mutual trust and cooperation between counselor and patient, in which the two work together as *equals* in the treatment process.

This applies to the educational setting as well. I often visit the schools I've founded and talk with students there. On one occasion, I was talking to a group of high school students who were in danger of failing. They seemed embarrassed, so I smiled broadly and told them that I had come to encourage them, not to scold them. After some friendly small talk about their health, their daily routines, and their families, I encouraged them to not let their poor grades get them down. I suggested they try to find one subject to excel in and to do their best to improve, one small step at a time, never giving up. I'm happy to say that my concern and advice helped, and all of them have turned their situations around, graduated with flying colors, and grown into fine adults. Some of them actually went on to become university professors.

MARINOFF: A very interesting story. In connection with therapy and education, this relationship of equals is independent of both the professional orientation of the counselor and the problem facing the client. It is dialogue itself that catalyzes the healing process.

Aside from Plato's dialogue *Thaetetus*, relatively few Western philosophical theories account for the healing effect of dialogue. Nonetheless, I have seen it work in practice over and over again. As you know, my books are full of case studies that richly illustrate this point.

We also find corroboration in case studies by Dr. Irvin Yalom, a brilliant pioneer of existential psychiatry. He explains that many of his patients are healed neither by artful psychoanalysis nor by insightful interpretations of their dreams but by his empathy, understanding, and nonjudgmental acknowledgment of their suffering. Thus the essence of healing, whether philosophical or psychoanalytic, seems to reside in empathic dialogue.

IKEDA: Dialogue is fundamental to Buddhism. For example, the compassionate Buddhist practice of eliminating pain and imparting joy that I have mentioned is carried out through dialogue.

In his final moments, Shakyamuni, who ranks with Socrates as one of the great teachers of humanity, urged his grieving followers to engage in dialogue with him. Up to the very moment of his death, Shakyamuni was inviting his followers to ask him—as one friend to another—anything they wanted to know.

The foundation of dialogue should be respect, empathy, and heartfelt, compassionate love for one's fellow human beings. Religion, like dialogue, is not a solitary activity. It should be a realm in which people protect and support one another, talking about their problems and encouraging one another.

MARINOFF: Dialogue plays a consistent healing role, whether in counseling sessions or larger group settings.

First, it encourages people to express themselves by allowing them to air their emotional discontent and conceptualize their circumstances.

Second, dialogue allows for alternative interpretations and constructive reformulations of such discontent and circumstances.

As an example, I counseled a successful professional woman trying to resolve a dilemma concerning career change. Her inability to make a choice was precipitating an emotional crisis. I firmly believed that in her heart she knew the right way to proceed, yet she was unable to articulate it to herself via introspective monologue. Our dialogue allowed her to behold a reflection of her mind and heart, whereupon she saw clearly what to do. She dispelled the crisis and resolved her dilemma by making a confident decision without regret.

Third, dialogue opens reflective space and liberates people from the emotional and conceptual burdens they habitually bear. All these things are conducive to healing.

Something Everyone Can Do

IKEDA: I agree completely with what you say of healing through dialogue. The human mind can be a maelstrom of hatred, greed, dissatisfaction, ignorance, mistrust, anguish, and insecurity. Again, Buddhism identifies negative mental states such as these as obstructions to enlightenment.

We also have positive mental states, such as compassion, wisdom, trust, hope, conviction, and self-control. The spiritual awakening that enables us to discover these positive states is called *bodhi*, meaning "wisdom" or "enlightenment."

Both the negative and positive states extend from the superficial levels to the deepest regions of the mind—and those that have been ingrained as mental habits starting in childhood are especially powerful.

Dialogue, by creating the reflective space you describe, is an opportunity for drawing out a person's positive mental functions and sharing them. It also brings the negative mental tendencies to the surface, into the light of day, where they can be consciously examined. This process enables people to perceive their situation with greater objectivity and to interpret the main cause of their suffering more constructively, empowering them to resolve and eliminate suffering. Such humane dialogue has never been as lacking as it is today—not only in medicine but in the home, the workplace, and the community as well.

At the foundation of good dialogue are the very positive mental functions that are then shared and reinforced in that reflective space. That's why a harmonizing, unifying force characterized by compassion, empathy, and mutual respect emerges in that space. This is what our society today needs most of all.

MARINOFF: Your insight is clear and deep. This is also why modern societies are responding so enthusiastically to Buddhism and philosophical practice alike. People feel too mechanized, institutionalized, bureaucratized, politicized, and ultimately dehumanized. Our work helps revivify humanity, reconnecting people to their inner resources and reawakening their natural capacity for wellness and the joy of life.

Perhaps we can expand even more upon this theme of dialogue by considering that the medium of spoken language necessarily utilizes sound waves. The human larynx is an incredibly sophisticated acoustic generator, and the human ear is adept at distinguishing niceties and subtleties of sound. We humans are truly a gifted species, having been vouchsafed among other gifts the power of the spoken word—that is, control of acoustic vibration. We have refined acoustic energy into enduring cultural expressions of oratory, poetry, music, and mantra.

IKEDA: This acoustic energy is very important. As Nichiren teaches, "Words are what give expression to the distinctions that are thought of in the mind."[3] Our voices, our words, are the reverberations of our thoughts, part of our inner world, manifested in the external world. These expressions of our minds then go on to play a part in various people's lives and in the larger culture.

We are not fully human at birth. Only through the training we receive in the sea of language, the sea of dialogue that constitutes our cultural heritage, do we acquire knowledge of ourselves, of others, and become fully human. In this sense, it can be said that dialogue is what makes us truly human.

MARINOFF: The problem is that the power of words can be utilized for ill as well as for good. All too often, language is abused to demonize, denigrate, or devalue others, all of which produce disunity. By contrast, dialogue can utilize the gift of language to harmonize, uplift, and value others, all of which produce unity.

Not every person is an orator, poet, or musician, yet every person can engage in dialogue, thus utilizing the gift of language to help unite humanity. A dialogue is like a dance with words. When people dance together, they experience unity.

"THE VOICE CARRIES OUT THE WORK"

IKEDA: Your comparison is very apt and clear. Dialogue is indeed a dance, a chorus, a performance.

My friend the world-famous musician Herbie Hancock shared an anecdote with me about performing in his youth with the great jazz virtuoso Miles Davis. Hancock once hit an obviously wrong note and couldn't think of how to recover from his mistake. Davis took that wrong note and incorporated it into the music, using it to create an even more wonderful performance. Hancock looks back on that moment with deep appreciation as a lesson that our apparent mistakes can be the building blocks of an even better life.

Dialogue really is to take action with the voice. With our voices, we praise, encourage, correct, heal, cheer up, and impart the energy of courage and hope. It is a dynamic exchange between one human being and another, one mind and another—always, it goes without saying, based on good will.

Buddhism teaches that "the voice carries out the work of the Buddha."[4] In other words, the voice awakens people to their inner enlightenment. That's how important the voice is regarded in Buddhism. The power of the voice of truth, brimming with formidable life force, is the Buddha in action, imparting peace of mind and stirring courage.

The motivating force behind dialogue should be a commitment to the absolute value of the individual. Through dialogue, we reinforce one another's positive mental states, deepen mutual understanding, and forge bonds of trust.

The Soka Gakkai International is based on such one-on-one dialogue. Through such dialogue, we support and expand positive mental states and the spirit of goodness within us all and build a network of friendship and solidarity to make the world a better place.

MARINOFF: Instead of merely espousing utopian ideals, the Soka Gakkai International is engaged in building a better world through dialogue.

I recently met and conversed with a number of youth leaders at the SGI-USA New York Culture Center. It was a privilege to encounter such a talented, well-educated, and highly motivated group of young people. They radiated not only goodness and solidarity but also boundless optimism, which cannot fail to inspire and uplift those with whom they interact. Your vision and example have engendered a generation of bodhisattvas whose harmonious voices create immeasurable value for those in direst need.

The Soka Gakkai International's mission is especially vital in this day and age since humanity is also exposed to inflammatory voices emanating from power-seekers who employ the ancient Roman maxim *Divida et Impera* (Divide and Conquer). Again, the power of words can be abused, fomenting conflicts instead of healing the world.

IKEDA: I am very grateful for your understanding of our movement. Our young people in America will be delighted by your comments.

As you say, modern society is filled with voices seeking to manipulate and divide people, using lies, slander, wild exaggerations, and insult to achieve their ends. In Nichiren's writings, we find the warning that "evil friends will employ enticing words, deception and flattery and speak in a clever manner, thereby gaining control over the minds of ignorant and uninformed people and destroying the good minds that are in them."[5] These voices are without a doubt a major cause of the sickness afflicting our society.

We need to take a resolute stand and eradicate, through the power of voices raised in truth, all these forms of harmful, malicious speech that are designed expressly to delude people and poison their minds. The Soka Gakkai's struggle over the years has in many ways been a struggle against this kind of falsehood and distortion—especially as it has appeared in parts of the Japanese media—that harms people and destroys society.

Decades ago, the outstanding Japanese educator Inazo Nitobe stated that Japan permitted abuses of speech to an extent rare among other nations. Nitobe was an under-secretary-general of the League of Nations and worked to build a bridge of amity across the Pacific connecting Japan and the United States. He was also on very friendly terms with Makiguchi, composing the preface for Makiguchi's groundbreaking work *The System of Value-Creating Pedagogy* (published in 1930).

In caustic criticism of the proliferation of irresponsible speech in the Japanese media of his day, Nitobe decried those in the press who made a living by ruining the lives and reputations of innocent, upstanding people. He also pointed out the collusion of the public, which allowed such attacks to go unchallenged and even encouraged them, treating them as a kind of sport.[6] Issued eighty years ago, this warning remains equally true today. We need to spread the voice of justice, truth, and hope—the voice that connects and enriches human minds. This is the only way to build a healthier society.

MARINOFF: Indeed, many of today's major media are even more powerful, corrupt, and out of control than they were in Nitobe's day. They titillate insatiable appetites for sensationalism and scandal. They distort, inflame, and mislead the masses at every juncture. They display the supreme arrogance of playing judge, jury, and executioner of anyone they decide to destroy.

In ancient Athens, Socrates observed that mass opinion vacillates like the wind, especially when people fail, for one reason or another, to calibrate their inner moral compasses. And after the masses turned on Socrates himself, leading to his execution, Plato wrote that the inflammatory media of his day (mostly oratory, poetry, and theater) needed to be censored by the State, for the good of the people themselves. Centuries later, in the New World, Thomas Jefferson was so appalled by the malicious broadsheets of his day that he refused to grant interviews, knowing his words would be twisted out of shape. This puts us in a real predicament, needing to find a Middle Way between State-controlled propaganda and flagrant abuses of free speech.

Nitobe was an amazing man, a Japanese Quaker who earned five doctoral degrees. His insights into Christianity, Bushido, and self-cultivation alike are profound and enduring. I am not surprised he was so close to Makiguchi.

As you and I have learned from Nitobe and Makiguchi, as well as from more ancient philosophers, we must always remain on guard against inauthentic, wounding diatribes delivered by demagogues and rabble-rousers who vainly seek to govern truth, instead of liberate people from falsehood.

Dialogue for Peace and Humanism

IKEDA: The United Nations proclaimed 2009—the fourth centennial of the astronomical observations of Galileo Galilei—the International Year of Astronomy. Looking up to the vast heavens above or into the deepest recesses of our own beings, we find unknown frontiers. Philosophy is the quest to explore these frontiers.

MARINOFF: Yes, it is: our innermost and outermost frontiers alike. As it happens, I visited the very house, in Florence, Italy, in which Galileo was born in 1564. What an inspiration! It perches on a hilltop with an expansive view of the town below and the heavens above.

On clear, cold winter nights, the glittering stars are like countless jewels scattered throughout the universe. Even living in noisy cities, people like to discourse with the stars of the nighttime sky.

IKEDA: The constellation Orion (the Hunter) shines especially bright in the winter skies of the Northern Hemisphere, sweeping from east to west. Sometimes called the monarch of the constellations, it has appeared in many myths and literary works since ancient times, inspiring feelings of poetic mystery and adventure.

The Orion Nebula—also known as Messier 42—is famous as a region of massive star formation. Recent studies have shown it to include a proto-planetary system similar to our Solar System. The drama of the birth and death of the stars unfolds on an immense cosmic scale.

MARINOFF: Orion has long enjoyed a special status, as it has persisted in its present form for about 1.5 million years—encompassing proto-hominid and human time on Earth. The Belt of Orion is used to locate two other important stars outside of Orion, namely Sirius and Aldebaran.

The cosmos is a mystical realm. Walt Whitman sings, "As I watch the bright stars shining, I think a thought of the clef of the universe and of the future."[1] Transient and tiny though we humans are, we can still contemplate the enormity of space and feel at home among its myriad stars.

IKEDA: Whitman's words resonate with the poetry of the great drama of the cosmos. A profound rhythm pulsates through past, present, and future, governing the movements of the cosmic bodies. I am certain that Whitman, with the sensitive soul of a poet, perceived this wondrous energy. One certainly feels the mysterious resonance between the immense cosmos and the inner universe of human life in his work.

MARINOFF: A spacecraft has been sent beyond our Solar System into the vastness of galactic space, bearing artifacts that represent the summit of human culture. It is hoped that an intelligent alien civilization will one day discover and decipher this cosmic "message in a bottle." One of the artifacts is a recording of J. S. Bach's music by pianist Glenn Gould.[2]

In a lecture at the SGI-USA New York Culture Center, I mentioned this spacecraft and suggested that we should send the Lotus Sutra into outer space. We humans must seek to propagate our noblest works throughout the galaxy, instead of squandering our vital energies in futile conflicts here on Earth.

IKEDA: What you say inspires great hope. As a matter of fact, in 2010, Soka University students in Japan developed and built a microsatellite named *Negai* (Wish), which was installed on a spacecraft set to explore the atmosphere of Venus. After a successful launch on May 21, 2010, the satellite was set in orbit, where it successfully completed its mission of about 500 rotations around Earth. Onboard the satellite were records of dreams and wishes collected from a large number of children. I think it is wonderful for the younger generation to get excited about space and the universe.

From a cosmic viewpoint, Earth is just one small planet, and the conflicts and wars of the human race are incredibly petty and senseless. Nothing is more important than peace, which should be our fundamental shared goal.

The astronomers and astronauts with whom I have engaged in dialogue have all shared the same idea. For example, the former cosmonaut Aleksandr Serebrov expressed his astonishment that, even in an age when we are capable of flying into space, humanity continues to squabble over little pieces of land on our small planet.

MARINOFF: Peace must be the cherished wish of all people. In our previous conversation (see Conversation Nine), we discussed the importance of dialogue from the standpoint of healing. This time, let's consider the significance of dialogue that, transcending cultural and religious differences, creates peace values.

A renowned dialogician, you have engaged in many dialogues with world leaders, Nobel laureates, and other prominent thinkers.[3] How have you managed to accomplish so much with so many, in such a large number of places, in such a relatively short time? Where did you make your start?

"Because There Are People There"

IKEDA: My first dialogue with a world thinker was with Count Richard Coudenhove-Kalergi.[4] We first met in October 1967, when I was thirty-nine. We continued to meet and talk, publishing our dialogue in 1972 (*Bunmei nishi to higashi* [Civilization, East and West]). In May of that year, my dialogue with Arnold J. Toynbee began.

MARINOFF: You conducted the dialogue at Toynbee's home in London?

IKEDA: Yes, I arrived at his red-brick apartment building at ten thirty in the morning on May 5, 1972, and took the elevator up to the fifth floor, where both Toynbee and his wife, Veronica, were waiting to greet me at the door with open arms. I remember the moment well.

It was in the fall of 1969 that I received a letter from Toynbee containing the courteous invitation to engage in a dialogue with him. I went to his home because of his advanced age. We spent a total of forty hours in discussions in 1972 and 1973, finishing in May 1973. I was forty-five years old at the time, and Toynbee was eighty-four.

As if imparting a cherished last wish to the next generation, he asked me to continue engaging in dialogue for the sake of uniting all humanity. Some time after our dialogue was finished, I received a hand-written note from Toynbee recommending such potential dialogue partners as Aurelio Peccei, founder of the Club of Rome, and microbiologist René Dubos, who was active at The Rocke-feller University. In a verbal message that he asked to be conveyed to me along with the note, he said: "These are my friends. I'm sure you have a busy schedule, but I know you'd find discussions with these individuals well worth your while." I took very seriously his wish that I continue trying to unite humanity through dialogue.

MARINOFF: You have maintained an attitude of thorough sincerity and even participated in dialogues with leaders and intellectuals from socialist nations, like China and the former Soviet Union. How can we convince non-dialogical partners—persons or peoples among whom communication has broken down and conflict has ensued—to initiate or renew dialogue?

IKEDA: Well, I believe it must start with human encounters. When I began my dialogue efforts, it was the time of the Cold War, and tension between China and the Soviet Union was high. But in my own way, I managed to open a path to dialogue—a path that Toynbee had so earnestly hoped to see open—with those nations. Many people at home and abroad criticized me, asking why a Buddhist leader should be visiting countries with ideologies unsympathetic to religion. I told people who came to the airport to see me off on those trips, "I am going because there are people there."

A hundred years ago, there was no such thing as a socialist nation. Human beings create social systems and ideologies, and those are always changing. I knew that, as fellow human beings, the people of China and the Soviet Union must want peace just as we do. We could come to understand one another, I was certain, if we persisted in frank and open dialogue based on our shared humanity. The path of friendship would open. This was the root conviction of my "personal diplomacy."

Nichiren teaches that "when one faces a mirror and makes a bow of obeisance: the image in the mirror likewise makes a bow of obeisance to oneself."[5] If you fully acknowledge the existence of others and treat them with respect, they will reciprocate. If you just dare to take that first step forward, the path of dialogue can be opened.

Once when I was in China, a charming little girl I met on the street asked what I had come to her country to do. I answered, "To see you." And I meant it. Prizing small encounters of that kind is what opens the way to friendship.

MARINOFF: Your practice of "personal diplomacy" has contributed significantly to dissolving barriers of xenophobic ideology, which divide humankind and impede human awakening. Moreover, you have set a compelling example by exercising such diplomacy not only beyond national borders but even through the Bamboo and Iron Curtains.

IKEDA: I'm afraid you overestimate my humble contribution. Nevertheless, communication does establish our common humanity, while refusing to communicate contributes nothing. As you just said, candid, heart-to-heart conversation can overcome xenophobia.

On our first trip to China, my wife was asked her opinion at our welcoming dinner. She said quite frankly: "In Japan, I had always been told that Communism is something to be feared. For that reason, I had come to perceive China as a scary country." Everyone tensely awaited what would come next. She continued, "After talking with all of you, however, I have come to see clearly that China is a warm country overflowing with love and humanity."[6] Her words were met with a round of applause, and we continued talking with a feeling of great openness on both sides.

MARINOFF: Gandhi and King both demonstrated the power of nonviolence and forthright dialogue within their respective nations; you have demonstrated it trans-nationally, among myriad nations.

The Buddhist metaphor you shared of bowing in obeisance in front of a mirror is illuminating. While the practice of prostration furthers the spiritual progress of adherents in many religions, including Buddhism, this reminds us that obeisance also serves the overarching purpose of uniting humanity itself. How many dialogical roads have you opened by means of your respectful approach and the reciprocity it engenders?

The Mentor-Disciple Relationship

IKEDA: In a sense, meeting great people and learning from their priceless experience and wisdom are worth more than reading mountains of books. I always make a conscious effort to learn as much as possible from free, open dialogue.

In the depressed period immediately after World War II, my mentor's businesses fell on hard times. When one after another, Toda's supposed friends and allies abandoned him, I stayed by his side and supported him, even setting aside my hopes to attend college.

To make sure that in the future I could hold my own in discussions with eminent leaders and scholars in any field, he gave me personal instruction in a full range of subjects, as I mentioned earlier (see Conversation Three). He always impressed upon me the "importance of sincerity, honesty, and remaining true to your beliefs." In my dialogues with world thinkers and leaders, I keep my mentor's spirit foremost in mind, and I feel as if he is always beside me, looking on. My joy now is expanding a network of beautiful, meaningful friendships in Japan and throughout the world, then turning this network over to the next generation.

MARINOFF: Your published dialogues are a bountiful source of education and inspiration to readers throughout the world. And your devotion to Toda is reminiscent of Plato's devotion to his mentor, Socrates.

Philosophy fell on hard times in ancient Athens, following the devastation of the Peloponnesian War and the execution of Socrates. Yet Plato's dialogues immortalized Socratic inquiry, and Plato went on to found the Academy, a model of higher education for leadership in every generation.

IKEDA: That's a very perceptive historical analogy: Plato's Academy is both the prototype of humanistic education and the archetype against which all education can be measured. The greatest philosophy, the greatest intellectual treasure, cannot be transmitted to posterity and spread throughout the world without education. It was the struggle of Plato, Socrates' student, that enabled his teacher's philosophy to shine throughout history. Together they illustrate a triumph of the noble mentor-disciple relationship.

MARINOFF: Similarly, you founded Soka University of America, Soka University of Japan, and the Soka schools. Both you and Plato played the great role of university founders. Beyond this, you nurtured the Soka Gakkai International into a humanistic religious organization that has swiftly spread worldwide. Although most global religious movements required centuries of evolution, you evolved the Soka Gakkai International's membership to comparable levels—millions of socially engaged members—in mere decades.

IKEDA: Celebrating the eightieth anniversary of its establishment in 2010, the Soka Gakkai is still very young. I believe that the organization's efforts, based on Buddhism, for peace, culture, and education will make an even greater contribution to humanity in the future. The Soka Gakkai International is an organization that brings people together through dialogue. It will continue to unite people's hearts and bring individuals, cultures, and countries together through one-on-one dialogue.

Our network for peace has spread to 192 countries and territories because of our commitment to inspirational dialogue. I hope, through dialogues with you and other leading world thinkers, to build a brighter future illuminated by a philosophy of peace, happiness, human revolution, youthful triumph, and respect for the dignity of life.

BUDDHISM'S SPIRIT OF DIALOGUE

MARINOFF: Nichiren laid the foundation for the kind of dialogue practiced by Soka Gakkai International members today.

IKEDA: Throughout his life, Nichiren was a committed practitioner of dialogue. He wrote many works in dialogue form. Perhaps the most notable in this category is "On Establishing the Correct Teaching for the Peace of the Land,"[7] a dialogue between a guest and a host. The guest is thought to represent the supreme political authority of the time, and the host is Nichiren.

It was a time of frequent earthquakes and climatic irregularities. The guest laments these natural disasters and their aftereffects, including widespread famine, epidemics, and a prevailing mood of fear and anxiety among the country's people. He also laments the general philosophical and religious confusion of the day.

The host agrees with the guest's assessment and proposes that the two of them sit and "discuss the question at length."[8] A frank dialogue ensues, and the host deplores the sufferings of the people, carefully outlining what steps the country's leaders need to take to bring happiness to the people and peace and security to society—while rebuking the leaders for failing to do so. Dialogue for the sake of the happiness of the people and world peace is the core spirit of "On Establishing the Correct Teaching for the Peace of the Land."

MARINOFF: I see. The Buddhist scriptures include many other works in dialogue form.

IKEDA: True. For example, I might cite *The Questions of King Milinda*, a dialogue between King Milinda (also known as King Menander), the Greek philosopher-king who controlled northwestern India in the middle of the second century BCE, and the Buddhist sage Nagasena. At the beginning of the work, Milinda asks Nagasena to talk together:

> The king said: "Reverend Sir, will you discuss with me again?"
>   "If your Majesty will discuss as a scholar (pandit), well; but if you will discuss as a king, no."[9]

No dialogue can be fruitful when either party approaches it with an arrogant attitude. True dialogue, Nagasena's reply indicates, cannot exist under the restraints of power and authority; it must be undertaken by two individuals on equal footing, jointly engaged in the pursuit of truth.

MARINOFF: Your point is vital and cannot be overstated. Literature from northern India and Tibet—Hindu and Buddhist alike—is replete with such reminders. From the *Ramayana* to seventeenth-century Buddhist fiction (e.g., *The Tale of the Incomparable Prince*), arrogant or cowardly words unfailingly ripen into bitter karmic fruit, bringing sorrowful ruin and painful awakening upon the utterers.

By contrast, words that emanate from sage minds illuminate truth and reality, bearing delectable karmic fruit not only for the utterers but also for the hearers. Minds that judge others on the

basis of social position or that are obsessed with differences between the conversing parties cannot communicate heart to heart.

IKEDA: In true dialogue, both participants must be prepared to put
aside their differences and relate to each other in a spirit of respect.
It doesn't matter with whom we're speaking, even a head of state.
To be successful, dialogue needs to be an exchange between equals
based on the recognition of shared humanity.

The Lotus Sutra presents a model for engaging in dialogue in the
figure of Bodhisattva Never Disparaging, whom I discussed earlier
(see Conversation Nine). As his name indicates, this bodhisattva
respects everyone. Knowing that the supremely respectworthy
Buddha nature resides in all people, he greets everyone he meets
with his palms joined in a gesture of respect. This causes some to
shun, revile, and persecute him. Nonetheless, he wisely remains
faithful to his nonviolent beliefs and continues his practice of respecting all others.

MARINOFF: The practice of Bodhisattva Never Disparaging, from
which we can learn much, indeed symbolizes the spirit of Buddhist
dialogue. To awaken happiness in others, we must encourage their
best qualities. Disparagement has the opposite effect; it demoral-
izes others and harps upon their worst qualities. Moreover, anyone
who works for the happiness of others must endure opposition
with equanimity. Isn't Nichiren a prime example?

IKEDA: Facing constant persecution and repeated exile, Nichiren
persevered tirelessly in his struggle to make the Buddhist teachings, aimed at the happiness of ordinary people, accessible to all.
Buddhist dialogue always takes the happiness of the ordinary people as its starting point. It is a humanistic practice that makes the
infinite potential in each individual's life shine its brightest.

The foundation of the dialogue conducted by Soka Gakkai

International members on a daily basis is prayer in harmony with the underlying law of the entire universe, the Mystic Law. This prayer contains a powerful determination, a vow or pledge, to break free of the chains of our personal karma and forge the way to happiness for ourselves and others.

Nichiren Buddhism teaches us how to carry out this life transformation that emerges from our firm determination; it is a philosophy of action. This is our practice of dialogue to achieve our human revolution.

I want to work with you, Dr. Marinoff, to make a bright sun of humanism rise over the horizon of our century and dispel the dark clouds looming over humanity today.

Ancient Questions, Timeless Wisdom

IKEDA: In March and April every year, when one class graduates from Soka University of Japan and a new one enters, the Hachioji, Tokyo, campus is fragrant with cherry, forsythia, and spirea blossoms. It was spring when you visited our university in 2007, and I hope the opportunity will present itself for another visit. When it does, I hope you will deliver a lecture to our students. I'm sure they would find it a source of great inspiration.

MARINOFF: Thank you very much. When I was at the Soka University campus for graduation ceremonies in March 2007, I was of course impressed by the beauty of the natural setting but also by the many handsome statues of such personages from the past as Victor Hugo, Walt Whitman, Leonardo da Vinci, and Marie Curie. It would be truly auspicious to deliver a lecture to your students in such inspiring surroundings.

IKEDA: On the campus of Soka University of America, we have a statue of Gandhi and a bust of Linus Pauling. The statues on our campuses represent great men and women who have made immortal contributions to the human race, people who in their respective fields—whether literature, the arts, science, or social activism—have embodied a firm philosophy of life, human existence, and peace.

Specialized knowledge is important, but it must be based on the foundation of a solid philosophy offering a profound view of the meaning of human existence. Such a philosophy is both a beacon enabling us to navigate the dark seas of life's long voyage and a compass charting a sure course through the turbulence of a rapidly changing society.

MARINOFF: As times change, the goals of human seeking, too, alter. When people tire of fads in entertainment, they seek something more. I think the best thing to seek is an unostentatious philosophy that sees life as it truly is. Everywhere and in all times, philosophy starts by questioning things. Instead of prescribing what to believe, it casts doubt, engendering healthy skepticism. Philosophical inquiry endeavors to discover—not to govern—truth.

IKEDA: I agree. The important thing, once again, is the ability to question. Asking the big questions awakens great wisdom. Such questioning transcends space and time.

In times of confusion and growing anxiety about the future, people turn to the wisdom of history in search of ways out of their predicaments. In both East and West, there have been repeated rediscoveries of and attempts to learn from the wisdom of classical thought and philosophy, such as the reawakening to the achievements of Greek and Roman thought during the European Renaissance. In recent years, in China, too, traditional philosophy has received a positive reevaluation. For example, in the latter half of the 1980s, Confucianism gained renewed recognition as a suitable subject of study.

The fact that your works on practical philosophy have become bestsellers around the world testifies to the thirst of people everywhere for a philosophy of life. Why we are born? Why does the world exist? Who are we? Though these may seem like naive questions, they don't have simple answers. This is what makes these questions so significant and eternal. Continuing to ask them is a sign, I believe, of the human race's tireless drive to better itself.

MARINOFF: And we had better be tireless. Each generation of scientists can add new layers to the scientific edifice, building atop what has been previously erected, but each human being begins his or her life journey at its very foundations. Thus, it is supremely important that we imbibe teachings from past sages.

It must be the duty of every government to inculcate virtues in its citizens, beginning at birth, so that they may attain their full moral stature as adults and serve as examples to their children in turn. The work of self-improvement is never done and must be constantly renewed—not only in every generation but in every waking moment of our lives. We must continually ferry immortal wisdom across time, from the past into the future.

RELIGION AND EDUCATION IN TANDEM

IKEDA: It is indeed our mission and duty as human beings to transmit a rich, vibrant heritage of wisdom to coming generations. The second-century Roman emperor and philosopher Marcus Aurelius writes:

> The lifetime of man is but a point; his being a flux; his perceptions faint and dull; his physical organism corruptible; his soul a vortex; his destiny inscrutable; and his fame uncertain . . . . What, then, can be our guide? Philosophy alone.[1]

When a single drop of water enters a great river, it attains eternal life; when we enter the river of the human spirit that is philosophy, we, too, gain a taste of eternity. The Roman philosopher Seneca writes, "Of all men only those who find time for philosophy are at leisure, only they are truly alive."[2]

This idea is shared by Buddhism. A life without conviction or philosophy lacks a foundation; without a foundation, it's impossible to build a life of value.

When Soka University of Japan opened (in 1971), I presented the university with a pair of bronze statues, masterful works of the nineteenth-century sculptor Alexandre Falguière. On the base of one of the statues, which depicts an angel and a printer, I had these words inscribed: "For what purpose should one cultivate wisdom? May you always ask yourself this question!" On the base of the second statue, which depicts an angel and a blacksmith, I had inscribed "Only labor and devotion to one's mission gives life its worth." These words express both my concept of the mission and responsibility of young people engaged in the challenge of learning and my belief in their infinite potential.

MARINOFF: Great works of art—such as those with which you have adorned the Soka University campuses in both Japan and the United States—are deeply symbolic of life, infused with the artist's inspiration and often with the patron's vision. To the celebrated philosophers of antiquity, life itself was an art form, and philosophy a guide to the art of living. It is most discerning of you to quote the Roman Stoics. They perceptively rediscovered many insights that were earlier realized and taught by Buddhist sages.

We cannot create value by accident: diligent effort and selfless devotion are necessary ingredients of any artful enterprise, including life. Yet the inner power of Buddhism transforms devotees' minds, so that the labor of creating value is never onerous but always joyous! Philosophical investigation is our guidepost to growth. Classical philosophies all perceived this. That's why a return to them is essential to human progress.

IKEDA: As we've discussed, modern society suffers from problems that include a loss of humanity and of any sound ethical compass. Nichiren, offering his view of history, speaks of an age "when good wisdom gradually diminished and evil wisdom surpassed it in people's hearts."[3] We're still living in that age today.

When used for ill, the human intellect only makes people unhappy. How can we deal with this dehumanization? In spite of regular calls for the restoration of humane values and fulfilling human relationships, we seem incapable of bucking the current of the times and generally at a loss for what to do.

MARINOFF: We live in an age in which—despite its marvels— dehumanization of many kinds is pervasive. One of its causes is the ongoing institutionalization of religious dogmas and the corruption of religious authorities, who ought to set models of good living.

Another is the rapid secularization of the world and the alienation of people from religion, to which normally they would turn. Mistakenly deifying computers and technology, which offer no moral guidance, they lose concepts of good and bad.

IKEDA: That's a very sharp observation. Religion should lead us in the direction of greater wisdom, strength, and goodness. Dogmatism, on the other hand, tends to enslave us and rob us of our ability to think. Unnoticed, teachings intended as the means to human happiness take on a life of their own and become ends in themselves.

I believe that intellectual strength and wisdom are essential if we are to prevent this from happening. This is why I always insist that religion and education must go hand in hand. In our age in which distinctions between good and bad are blurred, we must heed the words of wise thinkers of the past.

MARINOFF: Every human being, like every human culture, embodies the potential for greatness and terribleness alike. By tirelessly emphasizing human greatness as you do, you show people how much you value that which is great in them and their cultures. This not only enriches their lives directly but also has the effect of awakening their capacities to value the greatness of other persons and other cultures in turn.

There's no limit to the value that such mentorship can create, especially if its beneficiaries are exposed to this kind of thoughtful moral education from an early age. Otherwise, impressionable young people can fall prey to all that is terrible: deceitful prejudices and corrupted doctrines that deform, inflame, and enslave them. In every generation, wisdom is the only antidote to folly.

THE WISDOM OF THE CLASSICS

IKEDA: That's a very important point. In the speeches and essays I write for young people, I always try to share with them the writings and wise words of great thinkers from all ages and times. I introduce them to Confucius's philosophy of life, Socrates' determination to combat injustice, and Tolstoy's quest for the true nature of human existence. There's no end to the great thinkers from whom we can learn.

Toda always told me that "reading the classics and other great literature is indispensable in forming one's character and becoming a true leader." He would often ask what I was reading, what book I had finished that day. I also remember how strictly he would scold any young person he found reading worthless magazines: "What do you think you're accomplishing by wasting your time on such rubbish?"

When did you come to feel the need for the wisdom of classical philosophies in contemporary life?

MARINOFF: As I mentioned (see Conversation One), my convictions in this regard were formed initially in Vancouver during the early 1990s, where there emerged a grass-roots demand for philosophical guidance on a variety of personal and professional issues. That demand surfaced in Canada's ethos of universal and comparatively comprehensive education, health care, and social services. Even so, the practical wisdom of philosophy was missing from people's lives, as they themselves realized.

In the ensuing decades, my experiences in rendering philosophical services to people and organizations worldwide have only deepened my conviction that classical wisdom traditions play an essential role in improving the human estate and enriching the human condition.

To give some current examples, my American Philosophical Practitioners Association colleagues and I are working to bring practical philosophy to inmates of the US correctional system, to spinal-cord-injured patients in Sweden, to graduate students at a Catholic university in Taiwan, to women in Argentina, to political refugees from North Korea, to children in many countries who suffer from drug abuse, to young pioneers in biotechnologies, and to business leaders and civil servants from Europe and Asia.

IKEDA: Undeniably, the wisdom of classical philosophers has much to offer in helping us lead our lives as fully as possible today. It is a shining beacon of universal values. For instance, for Socrates, *arête*—excellence, or being the best you can be, often translated as "virtue"—was the supreme value.[4]

This and his belief in the immortality of the soul, transcending the end of our physical beings, enabled him to accept unjust condemnation and courageously drink the cup of hemlock. He believed that evil deeds leave a mark on the soul—an idea quite similar to the Buddhist teaching that our deeds, or karma, shape our lives throughout the three existences of past, present, and future. Both views recognize the eternity of being, transcending life and death in this present world.

MARINOFF: These are fine examples of how the Hellenic philosophers unwittingly reinvented many core precepts of Buddhism. Both Eastern and Western classical philosophies strove to articulate fundamental truths about human beings and our place and purpose in the cosmos.

Just as you say, Socrates willingly sacrificed his life to preserve his moral teachings for posterity. His student Plato taught that the human mind is powerful enough to apprehend eternal Forms, such as the immutable nature of Justice. Like Socrates, Confucius sought to transmit time-tested virtues to future generations. Like Plato, Lao Tzu attained consciousness of a domain beyond life and death, a domain from which all such apparent dualities arise.

As you know better than I, Buddhism probes these matters more deeply than any other philosophy known to humanity. Ultimately, there is neither East nor West: there is but one global village, inhabited by a unitary humanity.

IKEDA: In both East and West, philosophies that recognize the eternal nature of life have offered ethical foundations for society. In *The Republic*, Plato argues that a wise person who has studied philosophy—the so-called philosopher-king—should rule the state. The idea that those who govern should be followers of great philosophies is also found in Chinese thought, including, of course, Confucianism.

It is remarkable that several great thinkers seem to have emerged around the world at roughly the same time. Between 800 and 200 BCE, we see sophisticated philosophies emerging in India, China, and Greece. The origins of the majority of the great philosophies and systems of thought that exist today can be traced back to that time. Karl Jaspers called this the Axial Age.

MARINOFF: Yes, it is amazing. The Swiss psychologist Carl Jung proposed the idea of synchronicity to characterize phenomena that emerge at the same time in a meaningful manner but in the absence of causal interconnections. To me, the Axial Age represents the greatest leap forward ever in human consciousness. Everything humanity needs to know about leading fulfilled lives and creating continuity for subsequent generations was revealed by the sages of that period.

A matter of primary concern for philosophers in ancient Greek, Indian, and Chinese civilizations was defining the virtues that human beings should practice and the values they should espouse. I believe that these teachings came into being less because of Jungian synchronicity (which explains patterns after they emerge) and more because the world stood in need of them at that time.

You know the proverb "When the student is ready, the teacher will appear." Similarly, when civilizations are ready, sages appear. And when they do, they unfailingly further our development from animals into human beings and then into enlightened human beings. Thought is essential to the process.

IKEDA: As you keenly observe, thought is what makes us human. Concretely speaking, what does the capacity for thought tell us about being human?

THOUGHT IS NOT ENOUGH

MARINOFF: Thought is like a road map: it can set us, and sustain us, on the proper path to good and contributive lives. But thought is not enough. We also need to practice virtues in order to be fully human.

Since Buddhism combines religious and philosophical thinking,

I put it on a par with the philosophies of ancient Greece and Rome, and with Confucianism and Taoism. Indeed, Buddhism can be said to unite Western and Asian philosophies.

Aristotle emphasized self-realization through refinement of individual talents, whereas Confucius emphasized self-realization through sustenance of dutiful relationships. It seems to me that Buddhism in general and Nichiren Buddhist teachings in particular provide a synthesis of the best of Aristotle and Confucius.

You always encourage students to develop their individual talents so as to contribute to a better world. My attention was drawn to the Soka Gakkai International because your words include the philosophies of both East and West.

In recent years, Westerners have been attracted to ancient Asian thought, especially in relation to symbiosis with the environment. This, too, suggests that both Eastern and Western philosophies, if you dig deep enough, share common fundamentals.

IKEDA: Thank you for your understanding of our philosophical approach. Today, to deal with the world's environmental issues, we urgently need a philosophy that will provide a foundation for sustainable development and living in symbiosis with nature. A 2008 summit held on environmental issues[5] concluded that in order to make any progress in solving these problems, all nations need to work together, fundamentally rethinking our ways of living and organizing our societies. Without that, no solutions are possible.

MARINOFF: This means improving the relations between humanity and the environment in daily living. This, in turn, requires us to be aware of the necessity to fundamentally alter our habitual lifestyles.

IKEDA: Yes, it does. As I mentioned before (see Conversation Eight), Buddhism stresses the oneness of life and its environment.

Chinese thought, too, teaches that the human being and heaven—meaning the universe as a whole—are one. The underlying idea behind both thought systems is the connection between self and other, including the environment.

In a speech to the Chinese Academy of Social Sciences in 1992, I used the term *an ethos of symbiosis* to describe this common foundation. I said that the Asian tradition, which emphasizes harmony over conflict, unity over division, and "us" over "I," tends to seek a prosperity in which people live in symbiosis, a relationship of mutual support with other people and with nature. I believe that this way of thinking will make an increasingly important contribution to all humanity in the years to come.

MARINOFF: The Eastern emphasis on the unity of self and environment has spared Asian cultures many unwholesome effects of occidental dissociations.

In the West, Parmenides, founder of the school of Elea, articulated a corresponding philosophy in the fifth century BCE. He taught that our ordinary, piecemeal perceptions are mistaken, that the universe is an uncreated and indestructible whole, and that an eternal and unchanging reality underpins the apparent flux of phenomena. Parmenides' holism certainly influenced Plato.

IKEDA: In our dialogue, Toynbee said:

> A Westerner who has been educated in the Greek and Latin languages and in pre-Christian Greek and Roman literature finds [the oneness of life and its environment] familiar, because this was the *Weltanschauung* of the pre-Christian Greco-Roman world.[6]

I think this congruence can be seen as an example of the ideas that are common to many classical philosophies and thought systems. In later times, however, the idea that the self and the environment are separate assumed major prominence in the West, gaining ascendancy over the former view.

Atomism and Dissociations

MARINOFF: Yes, the Greek atomists, notably Leucippus and Democritus, proposed segmented and fragmented views, later echoed and amplified by Western science. With such noteworthy exceptions as the New England Idealists, Jan Smuts's fine book on holism,[7] and assorted holistic thinkers like Aldous Huxley and Arthur Koestler, Western philosophy and science evolved mostly along atomistic and dissociative lines, separating mind from body, self from society, man from nature.

Only in the late twentieth century, when the catastrophic effects of atomism and dissociation became palpable, did an alternative genre of Western philosophy and science begin to emerge. Engineer and innovator Buckminster Fuller coined the term *Spaceship Earth*, James Lovelock formulated the Gaia hypothesis (that living and nonliving entities comprise one single organism), and Rachel Carson founded the science of ecology with her book *Silent Spring*. And so the West began to rediscover the oneness of life and its environment.

IKEDA: All the people you mention have exerted a great influence on the modern environmental movement. Ideas like *Spaceship Earth* and the Gaia hypothesis have helped people recognize that the human race shares a common destiny. I'm delighted that many people today have to various degrees embraced these ideas.

MARINOFF: And they need to be even more widely embraced.

It remains to be seen whether China's current industrialization and accompanying environmental degradations reflect a wholesale abandonment of Confucian unity. Is China emulating the Industrial Revolution to its philosophical and environmental peril?

Are East and West now reversing their roles with respect to appreciation of the ideas of the oneness of humanity and heaven and the oneness of life and its environment?

IKEDA: Of course, each country has its unique situation with which to deal. At present, however, as one reflection of its current motto "A Harmonious Society," China is stressing environmental policies in keeping with the traditional Chinese concept of the oneness of humanity and heaven.

I have long advocated the creation of a Sino-Japanese environmental partnership. The environmental problems we face are urgent. With longstanding traditions that stress symbiosis with nature—and by cooperating closely and taking the initiative—Asian nations can make significant contributions to the amelioration of the world's environmental problems.

History shows that societies that forget or undervalue the wisdom of the past are headed for an impasse. In this connection, your efforts to revive the wisdom of classical philosophical traditions in the contemporary world and employ the illumination they offer us as individuals and societies are very significant.

MARINOFF: Thank you for saying so, but I'm only a finger pointing to the moon. Actually, your achievements in propagating both Nichiren Buddhism and outstanding ancient and modern philosophies deserve special note in modern history. After all, in one generation, your organization has expanded into a global network active in 192 countries and regions.

IKEDA: Your praise is too generous. This is all due to the efforts of the Soka Gakkai International members, who have striven tirelessly along with me.

Actual practice—action aimed at achieving peace and happiness for self and others—is the lifeblood of religion. Through our grass-roots movement, we of the Soka Gakkai International are eager to make contributions to social well-being. There is a pressing need to tap all the creativity and wisdom at our command so as to empower people everywhere to lead genuinely human lives. How can we exercise the wisdom to enable each individual to lead a worthwhile, meaningful daily existence? I'd like to further discuss the concept of "virtue" as an important model for answering this question.

On the Practice of Virtue

IKEDA: The month of May, with its gentle spring breezes, will be soon upon us (2009). The name for the fifth month in Japan's pre-modern lunar calendar is *satsuki*, written with a character representing an open vista drenched in light and meaning "bright," "high," or "expansive."[1] True to this image, May is a month filled with promise and vitality, a time of fresh growth for all living things.

MARINOFF: A single character brilliantly expresses a delicate sense of season. The English designations of each month derive from Latin words. For example, May comes from Maia, the Roman goddess of growth. The word *May* is also associated with vernal, green things.

In East and West, the month of May is associated with images of youthful, budding growth, rejuvenation, and an exuberant embrace of the coming summer. In his celebrated Sonnet 18, a tribute to enduring love, Shakespeare describes "the darling buds of May."

IKEDA: As I have said (see Conversation Ten), it was May when I visited Toynbee's London home for our dialogue. He had sent me a polite invitation: "I would like to welcome you warmly whenever you could come to London; however, I might suggest that some time next May would be a good time for us as we usually have a lovely spring in my country."[2]

Nichiren uses the metaphor of associating "with a friend in the orchid room"[3] to mean coming under the positive influence of a virtuous individual, just as being in an orchid-filled room perfumes you with the flowers' scent. I hope our dialogue will reflect just such an association.

MARINOFF: I share your sincere hope. Let's examine the meaning of virtue in human history, which I discussed in *The Middle Way*. I'd like to explore with you the subject of virtue as a condensation of the important models human beings need for living in the real world. Though the nature of virtue differs among cultures, each provides a standard evolved from daily experience for living a good life.

Ancient Greek philosophy, for example, prized the virtues of wisdom, courage, restraint, and justice. The Confucians respected the so-called five virtues: benevolence, justice, politeness, wisdom, and fidelity. Benjamin Franklin listed thirteen virtues: temperance, silence, order, resolution, frugality, industry, sincerity, justice, moderation, cleanliness, chastity, tranquility, and humility. We should respect all of these.

IKEDA: Historically speaking, many of these thoughts and philosophies were formulated in times of confusion and disorder rather than in times of social stability. The epoch creates the philosophy, and the philosophy responds to the epoch.

Nichiren writes of Confucianism:

Through these teachings, the people learned propriety and came to understand the debt of gratitude they owed their parents, and a clear distinction was drawn between the ruler and the ruled, so that the country was governed wisely. The people obeyed the leaders who followed those teachings.[4]

Sets of virtues, such as the ones you mentioned, were formulated in response to times of crisis, as guides for restoring humanity.

MARINOFF: This occurs time and again. Throughout history in both East and West, restorative works have been penned in response to dire crises. Lao Tzu wrote the *Daodejing* during the Warring States period (475–221 BCE); Plato wrote *The Republic* in the aftermath of the Peloponnesian War; Augustine wrote *City of God* after the sacking of Rome; Thomas Hobbes wrote *Leviathan* during the English Civil War.

In our times, Gandhi wrote *The Story of My Experiments with Truth* following India's struggle for home rule; Camus wrote *The Plague* in the wake of the Nazi occupation of Europe; you and Mikhail Gorbachev published *Moral Lessons of the Twentieth Century* after the thawing of the Cold War.

As mentioned in our previous conversation, human moral foundations cannot be taken for granted: they must be renewed in every generation. The foregoing examples serve to highlight how virtuous causes can and must be made, even—and especially—from the most dreadful circumstances.

IKEDA: The process you describe might be called the formula for human creativity and progress. Many of the great philosophers—including, of course, Socrates—who advocated the importance of virtues and themselves lived upstanding lives practicing the virtues they preached were reviled by their contemporaries. To-day as always, pointing out the correct, humane way of living can be a life-and-death struggle. This is an inescapable principle true in all times and places.

The Roman philosopher Cicero writes that

> equity, temperance, fortitude, prudence, all the virtues contend against iniquity with luxury, against indolence, against rashness, against all the vices; lastly, abundance contends against destitution, good plans against baffled designs, wisdom against madness, well-founded hope against universal despair.[5]

MARINOFF: It is true that established powers have targeted philosophers in every generation, censoring, persecuting, or even executing them for valuing truth and exposing falsehood, for promoting virtue and decrying vice, or for loving wisdom and correcting foolishness.

In 43 BCE, after denouncing the dictatorship of Marcus Antonius in his renowned *Philippics*, Cicero was beheaded. Antonius's wife, Fulvia, subsequently stuck a hatpin through Cicero's tongue, which shows how much they feared the power of his oratory. Yet such futile gestures could not eradicate the truth of his words.

IKEDA: No truly great person escapes persecution. In a lecture I gave at Soka University of Japan, "Thoughts on History and Historical Figures: Living Amid Persecution" (on October 31, 1981), I said that to be persecuted for one's beliefs is, in a sense, a supreme accolade and a mark of the highest honor.

Nichiren underwent a series of life-threatening persecutions because he taught Buddhism for the sake of people's happiness and spoke out for truth. He offered numerous explanations of the formula by which persecution operates—for example, "An evil ruler in consort with priests of erroneous teachings tries to destroy the correct teaching and do away with a man of wisdom"[6]; and "To practice as [the Lotus Sutra] teaches, and in accordance with the time and the people's capacity, will incite truly agonizing ordeals."[7]

How is the practice of virtue regarded today in the West, particularly in America?

MARINOFF: Having lived and worked in the United States since 1994, I have encountered a dire dearth of understanding and practice of virtue in American society. Europeans remain by far more cognizant of virtue than Americans. Holland, for example, has an annual Philosophy Month, whereas too many Americans never encounter philosophy at all during their lifetimes.

The City University of New York is on the verge of eliminating introductory philosophy as an undergraduate requirement. Thus hundreds of thousands of students in its dehumanized system will miss a vital opportunity to examine their lives through the lens of virtue.

Sadly, contemporary American culture is rooted in vice. Indeed, vice is glorified, sensationalized, celebrated, and rewarded. The economic collapse of 2008, which plunged the United States into recession and destabilized the global economy, was caused primarily by unrestrained avarice—systemic vice on a colossal scale.

Even the legendary homespun virtues of the American grass roots, whose praises were so eloquently sung by the likes of Tocqueville, Emerson, and Whitman, are being undermined and overwhelmed by rampant corruption in public and private sectors alike. The inevitable result is moral degeneracy and societal collapse.

As Toynbee writes, the "breakdowns of civilizations are not brought about by the operation of cosmic forces outside human control" but by "loss of mental and moral balance" in the values and conduct of their leaders and constituents.[8]

ONE VIRTUE ENTAILS ALL

IKEDA: Many Japanese thinkers and commentators have suggested that, unfortunately, our nation also lacks a sustaining philosophy of life. Which of the various virtues enumerated by philosophy since ancient times do you consider especially significant for society today?

MARINOFF: All the classical virtues have special meaning for every generation. What they hold in common is the guiding idea that human nature is malleable. Since human nature is fundamentally and universally one thing—differing languages, beliefs, customs, and cultures denoting only cosmetic dissimilarities—all virtues must be common to all humanity.

It is clear—from both theoretical and practical standpoints—that courage, justice, wisdom, and temperance are interrelated. The exercise of any one entails the exercise of them all.

IKEDA: These are very important points, especially the idea that the practice of one virtue entails the practice of all of them. This, it seems to me, is a core truth when considering philosophy.

As the Greek poet Theognis of Megara says, "In justice is all virtue collectively, yea, and every man, . . . if just, is good."[9] Achieving justice requires courage, action, and wisdom. And one must acquire the strength to stand against misfortune and evil. Numerous virtues are encompassed in the acts of standing up for, speaking out for, and accomplishing justice.

Philosophy, again, shouldn't be seen as a pursuit reserved for professional philosophers. It's a process in which anyone can engage as they try to deal with the questions that arise in their daily lives.

MARINOFF: The quest for virtue in a vicious world, however arduous the path and seemingly distant the goal, begins in each person's mind at this very instant. People need not await the coming of saviors or the anointing of philosopher-kings; rather, everyone can exercise virtue at any time and place, thus contributing to a better world here and now.

Shakyamuni's last words reportedly exhorted his followers in just this way: "Work out your own salvation with diligence."[10] Everyone can follow their own inner light—especially when practicing the virtues that make it shine most brightly. For lives thus illuminated, no journey is wearying, no path obstructed, no sorrow debilitating, no evil triumphant. Aristotle taught that we attain justice by performing just acts, that we practice courage by doing courageous deeds.

IKEDA: Action comes first. Toda often said that "no matter who tries to stand in their way, young people need to fight courageously." I remember him saying to me: "Pay no attention to those who demean or ridicule you; just press forward to your goal. Rely on the strength provided by your Buddhist practice." I, too, constantly urge young people to act with courage.

Righting injustice demands courage. Encouraging friends with problems is an act of kindness based on the often unrecognized courage it takes to reach out to others.

In a sense, even getting up early in the morning requires courage! Overcoming one's weaknesses takes courage.

Acquiring knowledge of virtue is not necessarily acquiring virtue. Putting that virtue into action—praxis—is necessary. As Marcus Aurelius writes: "Waste no more time arguing what a good man should be. Be one."[11] That's why the existence of a mentor acting along with young people, offering them a model, is so important.

A STRONG, UNSHAKEABLE SELF

MARINOFF: Your mentor, as well as the Stoic philosophers, reconstituted the key insight of virtue ethics, which Aristotle had elaborated in 350 BCE (in *Politics*, written that year): that we become good not merely by contemplating the nature of goodness but rather by acting habitually in accordance with virtue. Aristotle also required courage to espouse this view, for it directly contradicted Plato, who taught that we become good by apprehending the form of goodness.

That's why Aristotle was not selected to succeed Plato as head of the Academy and was obliged to found his own school, the Lyceum. Raphael's celebrated painting, *The School of Athens*, which we have already had occasion to discuss (see Conversation Six), portrays this schism in an inclusive and possibly ambivalent light, granting equal footing to both views.

How does Buddhism interpret virtue?

IKEDA: One example would be the four virtues that are the characteristics of bodhisattvas and Buddhas—eternity (*jo*), happiness (*raku*), true self (*ga*), and purity (*jo*). Eternity refers to the constant presence of the Buddha nature inherent in all living beings. Happiness refers to enjoying a life of great vitality. True self is the establishment of a firm, indestructible identity, the greater self surpassing our petty, limited egos. Purity is acting with a mind of pure and undefiled goodness even within the mire of the real world.

Buddhism is not abstract theory. The purpose of our Buddhist practice is to build a self that can stand strong and unshakeable, like a treasure tower (an image from the Lotus Sutra). It stands in the face of the universal sufferings of birth, aging, sickness, and death while embodying these four virtues of eternity, happiness, true self, and purity. By changing ourselves, we change our environment and move onward and upward along the path of a good life. This is the meaning of human revolution.

MARINOFF: This is precisely why Buddhism can be understood as an applied philosophy centered in virtue ethics. The profound and excellent goal of changing the environment by altering the self is applicable to all people.

In ordinary counseling, I offer philosophical prescriptions, but the sicknesses causing suffering are incredibly numerous and diverse. If I were aware of a prescription that could function as a panacea across the broad spectrum of ills afflicting humanity, I would not hesitate to enunciate it. For the majority of those who seek meaningful and beneficial ways of life, I would prescribe some version of the Middle Way. As you know, I dealt extensively with this issue in *The Middle Way*.

IKEDA: I understand that your book has been well received not only in America but also in Spain, Italy, England, China, and elsewhere. I'm grateful for the autographed copy of the Chinese edition you were kind enough to send me. My Chinese friends, too, have been very impressed by *The Middle Way*.

MARINOFF: I'm happy to hear it. In the United States, a number of intellectuals and radio hosts have praised it highly, as did *Library Journal*. I have adapted part of the book ("American Gulag" from Chapter Eleven) for a documentary film, and other parts may be adapted for a TV series. A number of producers and directors have expressed interest in adapting *The Middle Way*.

As I mention in the book, the encouragement and sincere opinions you provided helped me greatly to complete it.

TRUE MEANING OF THE MIDDLE WAY

IKEDA: You are too kind. I am happy to have been of some small assistance.

You say that you had two aims in writing the book. First, you wanted to use the philosophies of Aristotle, the Buddha (Shakyamuni), and Confucius to moderate the ideological extremes that incite the world to collision and conflict. Second, you wanted readers to use these philosophies, these ABCs, to solve their individual problems.[12]

Aristotle taught the golden ratio between extremes, and Confucius emphasized the importance of the doctrine of the mean, of moderation. But in Buddhism, the "Way" of the Middle Way specifically refers to *practice*. The essence of the Middle Way is to follow the Way or "practice between extremes"—to *put into practice* the fundamental principle that pervades the universe and all life.

MARINOFF: Aristotle, Shakyamuni, and Confucius all taught that the virtue of moderation is a key to happiness and fulfillment, whereas vices of excess and deficiency lead to unhappiness. They all insisted that virtues must be practiced on a daily basis. Likewise, they taught that certain actions—such as murder, theft, calumny— are inherently wrong, thus exceptions to the rule of moderation.

One shortcoming of Aristotle's virtue ethics is its lack of extended and advanced instruction for daily practice, while Confucian traditions often succumb to the pitfalls of rote and unreflective learning. I find no such shortcomings in Buddhism. It teaches powerful practices and, owing to its universal humanistic foundations, can be followed by all people—even those with theistic religious beliefs.

In this sense, it is superior to the thought of Aristotle and Confucius; it accommodates the strengths of both while resolving the fundamental tension between them. Aristotle favors the individual over the group; Confucius, the group over the individual. Buddhism asserts the value of every sentient being yet emphasizes the interconnectedness of all beings.

IKEDA: Yes, that's correct. More specifically, Buddhism teaches the eightfold path.[13] Shakyamuni taught that the three poisons of greed, anger, and foolishness are the cause of the suffering we experience when confronted with the realities of birth, aging, illness, and death. He taught the eightfold path as the practice for breaking free from the three poisons and attaining a state of indestructible happiness, or nirvana. The eightfold path elucidates the correct life, the practice of the Middle Way separate from the extremes of the ascetic rejection of all desires and hedonistic attachment to them.

Mahayana Buddhism spread the idea of the bodhisattva who strives for the enlightenment of self and others at the same time. A system of practice was also articulated, specifically for the bodhisattva: the six *paramitas*,[14] the first being the giving—in a broader sense, contributing to the happiness of others—that we touched upon earlier (see Conversation One). The four virtues of eternity, happiness, true self, and purity that I mentioned are the virtues manifested as the bodhisattva puts into practice the six *paramitas*.

The basic meaning of the Middle Way is to make the incomparable treasure inherent in all life shine—that is, to manifest the supreme worth and dignity of what we might call the Life with a capital "L" within one's own life. This is the model of humanism in Buddhism.

MARINOFF: Thank you for delving more deeply into the virtues of the Middle Way. During your long and distinguished leadership of the Soka Gakkai International, you have carried the Buddhist idea of the Middle Way all over the world, into many countries and cultures. Have you encountered objections to it?

IKEDA: Because of both international and local political situations, there have been, at times, some who regarded the Soka Gakkai International with suspicion. This was based on misunderstanding and fear—for example, seeing us as a "foreign" religion with a hidden agenda. There was resistance in some Asian nations in particular, resulting largely from their history of having been subjected to Japanese military aggression.

But as people learned of the courageous struggle of Makiguchi and Toda against the wartime militarists and gained a deeper understanding of our Buddhist philosophy of respect for the worth and dignity of life, appreciation and acceptance of our movement grew. Through the sincere, persevering efforts of Soka Gakkai International members around the world, working with their fellow citizens for the happiness of all and the peace and prosperity of their societies, we are winning the solid trust of the public.

The Soka Gakkai International was officially founded during an assembly of representatives from fifty-one nations and regions held on Guam in January 1975. On that occasion, I said: "Rather than seeking after your own praise or glory, I hope that you will dedicate your noble lives to sowing the seeds of peace of the Mystic Law throughout the entire world. I shall do the same."[15] I firmly believed that, though we might encounter hostility at first, the Mystic Law and our movement would and must finally win understanding. Now the sun of Nichiren Buddhism shines throughout the world.

Our members proceed along the broad path of humanism in keeping with the Middle Way and, as good citizens of their countries and the world, work for peace, culture, and education wherever they live. Our young people, who shoulder the future, embrace a sound philosophy of hope and respect for the worth and dignity of life and, motivated by a powerful sense of mission, are working hard to make a positive contribution to society.

FRIENDSHIP AND VIRTUE

MARINOFF: You demonstrate a strong and pervasive sense of optimism. I know that people all over the world support and share your unwavering adherence to the Middle Way. I have met Soka Gakkai International members from and in many countries, who work ardently to actualize your vision.

By contrast, it is sometimes difficult to prescribe what is most essential for people who have neglected their philosophical development. I have seen many instances in my counseling practice in which the roots of clients' problems lie in unwholesome attachments of various kinds.

For example, they may take to drink, demonstrate an insatiable desire for success, become mistrustful or angry, or seek refuge in escapism. The Middle Way offers the most effective means for dissolving such attachments and indicating the path they should follow. Clients benefit greatly from the philosophy of the Middle Way, provided they are prepared to assume appropriate measures of responsibility for their suffering and its alleviation.

IKEDA: Yes, the attachments of which you speak are, again, what Buddhism calls obstructions to enlightenment, starting with the three poisons (greed, anger, and foolishness). The practice of the Middle Way—in the form of the six *paramitas* and the eightfold path—is the practice for breaking through those obstructions.

By adopting a life based on the Middle Way in order to overcome suffering, we transcend the small self, captive to its fleeting desires and delusions, and move toward a life based on the greater self of the bodhisattva, who is engaged in relieving the sufferings of others. Buddhism teaches that the right way to live is to realize one's full potential, make the effort to reach out to others, and together with others open the way to happiness and triumph in life for all. This is the practice of the Middle Way.

MARINOFF: The bodhisattva's altruistic way of life is a model for all humanity. Nichiren's philosophy is permeated with absolute respect for others.

One of the most outstanding elements of Mahayana Buddhism is the teaching of converting one's sufferings into a force to help others. Surely, the wisdom of Buddhism, with its emphasis on direct human interaction, deserves great attention in this age when impersonal, anonymous contact via the Internet trivializes, distorts, and impoverishes human relations.

For example, young people these days are led to believe that they can make a "friend" online by simply clicking on a link with a mouse. But this is potentially a form of social impairment that utterly neglects awareness and practice of the virtues of friendship (as elegantly extolled by Aristotle in his *Nichomachean Ethics*). A young person may thus "make" a thousand "friends" on Facebook without ever experiencing one single meaningful human contact.

IKEDA: Human beings cannot live without involvement with other human beings. In today's society, however, we exploit, commercialize, and discriminate against one another in ways that increasingly destroy human relations.

How can we live lives of value? How can we live good, meaningful lives? In today's harsh, barren society, which has lost sight of the criteria for answering these questions, we are searching for a way to reawaken our shared humanity and the strength to make our lives meaningful and worthwhile. In this context, I see enormous potential in the practical-philosophy movement, which brings people together in inspiring, revitalizing dialogue to overcome life's many challenges and problems.

The Arts and the Human Spirit

IKEDA: Music is the sound of progress, the rhythm of hope, and the voice of peace.

In January 2009, Argentine tango master Osvaldo Requena performed in Japan under the auspices of the Min-On Concert Association. To my honor, he presented me with two works of his own composition at that time. I have a very pleasant memory of listening to these pieces with a large group of young people. All our hearts were stirred by the lively rhythm of the tango—so much so that some of my young international friends visiting Japan actually got up to dance.

Music has the power to transcend national and linguistic boundaries, harmonizing, uplifting, and unifying human hearts. From my youth, even when very busy, I have always tried to make time to listen to Beethoven, one of my favorites, and other works of classical music, seeking inspiration in great art. I know that you, too, are very fond of music. What are some of your favorite works?

MARINOFF: Music has always been vitally important to me. As a young man, I earned a living performing and teaching music.

Beethoven composed powerful and immortal works, to be sure. My favorite period is the high Baroque (1700–50), which saw a flowering of great composers, including Handel, Scarlatti, Telemann, Vivaldi, Weiss, and above all Bach. To me, Bach's works are the most beautiful and sacred in the Western canon—and also the most challenging to play.

Spiritual contact with great art in everyday life has an enriching influence. In the United States, numerous musical events occur toward the end of May, the beginning of summer and the time when the nation honors its war dead on Memorial Day. It is wonderful that opportunities to experience culture and art increase during the expansive mood of summer.

IKEDA: Yes, in perfect harmony with the wondrous rhythm of the four seasons. Art is the light of humanity and the brilliance of life. A world without it would be a spiritual desert. It is in the arts that the human spirit can soar freely.

The Lotus Sutra describes the realm in which the Buddha eternally abides as a place where

> jeweled trees abound in flowers and fruit
> where living beings enjoy themselves at ease.
> The gods strike heavenly drums,
> constantly making many kinds of music.[1]

This description testifies that Buddhism, far from being the joyless, life-negating religion that some imagine it to be, has a deep appreciation for both life and music.

The great eighth-century Chinese Buddhist priest Miaole (Zhanran, sixth patriarch of the Tiantai school) writes in *The Annotations on "Great Concentration and Insight,"* "First the teachings on propriety and music were set forth, and later the true way was introduced."[2] In other words, at least to a certain degree, the spread of rites, music, and the arts prepares the way for and helps promote a grasp of positive social ideals and philosophical truths. Music and the rest of the arts can exert a very powerful influence on both the individual and society. A single piece of great music or a masterpiece painting has the power to elevate the human spirit tremendously. Great art and great philosophy work together on a profound level to foster human creativity.[3]

MARINOFF: As you rightly observe, Chinese philosophical traditions are replete with reverence for music. In its explication of the sixteenth hexagram—Yu (Enthusiasm)—the *I Ching*, or *Book of Changes*, says that the ancient kings made music at the beginning of the summer to honor merit as a splendid sacrifice to the Supreme and invited their ancestors to be present.[3] Music was the catalyst for aligning the mystical forces that govern the universe. Confucius says of this rite, "He who could wholly comprehend this sacrifice could rule the world as though it were spinning on his hand."[4]

In general, creative artists—poets, authors, composers, painters, sculptors—drink from a common well of universal wisdom. Plato called creative art *mimesis*; that is, "representation." He meant that nothing is actually created and that artists *represent* vital aspects of eternal wisdom, beauty, harmony, or geometry. The more deeply an artist drinks from this well, the more universality is reflected in the art itself.

We find the spirit of the American people reflected in Whitman's poetry. We find the eternal wisdom of Hellenic philosophy reincarnated in the Italian Renaissance. And we find the practical wisdom of Nichiren Buddhism reflected in the contemporary jazz of Herbie Hancock, Wayne Shorter, and Larry Coryell.

IKEDA: Yes, that's very true. These jazz musicians you just named are striving, with Buddhism as their source of creative inspiration, to promote peace and to bring hope and courage into people's lives.

Rules and Rhythms of the Cosmos

MARINOFF: During the writing of *The Middle Way*, I discovered that when one contemplates wisdom from the standpoint of universal constants, the cosmos seems to possess rules and rhythms. Moreover, it turns out that the geometry of the lotus flower also incorporates one very special universal constant, φ, known as the golden ratio.[5]

The iconography of the three wisdom traditions of Aristotle, Shakyamuni, and Confucius are inextricably linked by a geometric constant woven into the fabric of the universe itself and related to regularity and artistic rhythm. It would be interesting to contemplate the mantra *Nam-myoho-renge-kyo*,[6] chanted by believers in Nichiren Buddhism, in light of its resonance with universal constants.

IKEDA: I understand the point you're making, and you're quite right. I believe there is a principle that pulses within the universe, a rhythm with which all things reverberate. As Nichiren puts it, "If you think the Law is outside yourself, you are embracing not the Mystic Law but an inferior teaching."[7] All the laws and principles that exist throughout the universe also permeate the innermost depths of the individual—this is the truth that Buddhism has apprehended and teaches.

I'm reminded of my meeting with the celebrated violinist Yehudi Menuhin. When we met in Tokyo in April 1992, we discussed a wide range of topics from life philosophy to music. He told me that all people can "directly contact and harmonize themselves with the vibrations of the universe."[8] He also said that an SGI-UK member had taught him *Nam-myoho-renge-kyo*. Menuhin remarked on "the wonderful rhythm that is Nam-myoho-renge-kyo"[9] and that he himself hummed it practically every day. "The fact that people regularly chant Nam-myoho-renge-kyo each day is indeed wondrous," he added.[10]

MARINOFF: Menuhin's reaction and comments provide ample food for thought. He was a gifted violinist and brilliant interpreter of music in a century that saw the instrument elevated to new heights of virtuosity by a pantheon of prodigies. I still enjoy listening to Menuhin's recordings, including some of his earlier ones, such as the evocative "Songs My Mother Taught Me" by Antonin Dvorak. Menuhin also performed a great service in uniting the classical traditions of East and West in his amazing recordings with the celebrated sitarist Ravi Shankar (*West Meets East*, 1999). Playing together, they teach us that music is a celebratory common denominator of all human cultures.

IKEDA: I'm very happy to learn that you, too, deeply love Menuhin's music. I also remember Menuhin saying that music is a source of constant encouragement and cheer, even in the most trying of times. As you've said, from ancient times, music has been regarded as a manifestation of the harmony of nature. Mathematics, music, and all fields of learning and art, as well as every great thought system and philosophy, are attempts to express and illuminate the principle that animates the universe, the harmonizing rhythm of all existence.

MARINOFF: The Pythagorean tradition from ancient Greece emphasized the deep connection among geometry, music, and philosophy. Proportionality, harmony, and balance are essential features not only of great art and architecture but also of greatness in human thought, character, and society. In exactly this context, Aristotle conceived of politics and statecraft as the highest art forms, as did Lao Tzu and Confucius in ancient China.

Pythagoras may have been influenced by Indian philosophy. In any case, it is worth noting that the Indian "ladder" of yogas—starting with hatha yoga and leading, rung by rung and century by century, to the most esoteric practices of Buddhism—recognizes yantra yoga (the yoga of geometric forms) and mantra yoga (the yoga of acoustic vibrations) as immediate neighbors and therefore as closely related families of practices.

It is clear to me that you have also expressed this vital linkage among geometry, music, and philosophy in your lifework. You are an accomplished poet and photographer. You have also made great music and art from around the world accessible to the public through your founding of the Min-On Concert Association and the Tokyo Fuji Art Museum, both of which I have had the privilege of visiting and admiring. You consistently attribute your remarkable artistic inspiration and vision to your mentor, Toda, and to his mentor, Makiguchi.

WE ALL NEED ROLE MODELS

IKEDA: You're very kind to say so. I owe everything to my mentors. Without these two great teachers, the Soka Gakkai International would never have grown into what it is today, and our peace, culture, and education activities would never have developed globally. I have always put my mentors' teachings into practice in my life and have struggled to create the kind of future they envisioned. I consider this the most admirable way of living as a human being. Nichiren writes that one "owes a profound debt to one's teachers for preventing one from following erroneous doctrines and leading one to the correct way."[11] We all need, in one form or another, teachers who serve as role models instead of merely dispensing knowledge.

Who are some of the teachers you most respect?

MARINOFF: At every stage of my life, in both academic and non-academic settings, I have encountered mentors of many kinds. I believe strongly in the Confucian precept that we can learn something from everyone we meet, in any station of life. How much more, then, can we learn in formal mentorship contexts!

Teachers who have most influenced me include the late Douglas Lawley, Latin master at Lower Canada College and an eminent painter of wild horses; Grandmaster Sing Ming Li, founder of the Wu Do Kan Kung Fu Academy in Montreal; Professor Elaine Newman, founder of Science College at Concordia University; and Professor Klaus Schwab, founder of the World Economic Forum.

I have also been privileged to learn from great classical guitar teachers and performers, including Miguel Garcia, Florence Brown, Peter McCutcheon, Alexander Lagoya, Harold Micay, and David Leisner.

My Buddhist mentors have included Sogyal Rinpoche (Tibetan Dzogchen tradition), Roshi Robert Kennedy S. J. (Zen Soto tradition), and, since 2002, you and your Soka Gakkai International colleagues in the Nichiren tradition.

As the fruits of the mentor-disciple relationship gradually ripen, they produce inexpressible joy, profound gratitude for the benefits of lifelong learning, and a personal obligation to mentor others.

IKEDA: As can be seen by looking at many of the figures whose names have gone down in history, the existence of a mentor-disciple relationship plays an important, definitive role in human life.

Because of the mentor-and-disciple relationship between Socrates and Plato and between Plato and Aristotle, the wisdom of ancient Greece has been passed down to the present, still inspiring and illuminating us. Plato founded the Academy and Aristotle the Lyceum—clear indications that they placed high priority on fostering students to carry on their intellectual legacy.

We can identify a similar relationship between Confucius and his followers. The *Analects* depicts a beautiful mentor-and-disciple relationship, with Confucius's followers revering their teacher in their role as the inheritors of his thought.

In Buddhism, Shakyamuni's disciples collected his teachings as the Buddhist scriptures and transmitted them to the present. First Soka Gakkai president Makiguchi, second president Toda, and I, the third president, all followed this path of mentor and disciple, transmitting a shared commitment to justice and peace.

MARINOFF: I understand that Makiguchi died in prison.[12] His death must have been a tragic blow for Toda. Socrates' imprisonment and death had similarly profound effects on Plato.

As you know, Thoreau, Gandhi, and King, too, were imprisoned at various times for civil disobedience and "made good causes" with their imprisonments. What similarities do you see in the imprisonments of humanity's greatest mentors?

IKEDA: Those who fight for justice are persecuted—that's an immutable rule of history. The strength to overcome persecution and persevere in the course of justice comes from the mentor-disciple bond.

Tagore writes:

> Did those who listened to the great teacher merely hear his words and understand his doctrines? No, they directly felt in him what he was preaching, in the living language of his own person, the ultimate truth of Man.[13]

Learning the ultimate truth of existence from the teacher's words and actions—this, I believe, is the essential point of the mentor-disciple relationship.

Having apprehended and learned how to live a good life, the student or disciple naturally feels gratitude and strives to repay his or her debt to the mentor, as well as to carry on the mentor's vision. The drive to repay one's mentor can be a powerful source of strength to overcome any obstacle or difficulty.

I firmly believe that the mentor-and-disciple relationship is the axis of both humanistic education and value creation. The mentor doesn't simply transmit a body of knowledge to the student; the mentor's effort, summoning every iota of his being, to train and inspire the student plays a decisive role in the formation of the student's character and his or her growth as a human being.

Both Makiguchi and Toda were schoolteachers. Makiguchi took Socrates' educational methods as a model for the humanistic education he advocated. He admired Socrates for his emphasis on the inquisitive spirit of self-examination—"Know thyself"—and his active engagement in dialogue and exchange with the young. I believe that you, too, put great importance on dialogue with the young and on raising leaders.

Students Come First

MARINOFF: Indeed, I do! As a beneficiary of inspired teaching, I aspire not merely to impart knowledge but also to awaken the powers of my students' minds. This can be accomplished only via person-to-person interaction, personal example, and dialogue. Even the greatest libraries of the world, or the vast storehouses of data on the World Wide Web, cannot rival the teacher-student relationship. The instantaneous chat rooms on the Internet, which allow people to communicate virtually across great distances, likewise fail to embody the vital dimension of real human contact, for which there is no technological substitute.

What is your guiding educational principle?

IKEDA: That students come first. The educator, having been entrusted with students and with the task of helping each of them make the most of their lives, has a heavy responsibility. He or she must be entirely devoted to the students' growth and future. And he or she must never condescend to or belittle them under any circumstances. It's important to trust and respect the individuality of even the youngest primary-school pupils. This kind of one-on-one, life-to-life interaction develops a sense of self-confidence and self-knowledge in children.

Most important of all, the teacher must impart the indomitable spirit to face life's tempests with composure. People can't be happy without inner strength. We can imbibe information from books and texts, but information alone won't overcome life's challenges.

In addition, teachers need to instill the importance of peace in their students. I'm a member of a generation that experienced war; I have had more than my share of the misery of war, brought on by the follies of militarism. This is why, as my life's last major task, I have devoted myself to education for the sake of peaceful living, in keeping with the best of which human beings are capable.

MARINOFF: The way you have founded numerous educational institutions all over the world in such a relatively short time is truly praiseworthy. Having visited Soka University of America on several occasions, I must congratulate you for having founded such a thoroughly impressive institution. I suspect that its students and alumni will thank you for a long time to come.

Soka University of America elected to be a liberal arts college. Speaking both as a beneficiary of a liberal arts education and as a contributor to such programs, I have come to regard liberal arts as a cornerstone of Western civilization and modernity, and therefore indispensable to any enlightened vision of the global village.

IKEDA: I am deeply grateful to the leading intellectuals from all over the world, such as yourself, who have visited Soka University of America to encourage our students. Many of our Soka graduates are doing pioneering work in their fields the world over. Every day, I receive letters from Soka alumni. Nothing delights me more than hearing of their successes.

The value of a university is measured by its graduates. Our alumni, who continue to strive to be the best people they can be, filled with pride in their alma mater, are the university's greatest treasure. I have the highest praise for them.

Soka University of America is still a young institution. What words of advice do you have for it?

Universities in the Twenty-first Century

MARINOFF: The mission of a university education in the twenty-first century must be to carry on the study of and foster further contribution to what Matthew Arnold called "the best which has been thought and said in the world"—across the spectrum of knowledge. Beyond this, the prominent theme must be the inculcation of virtues compatible with the emergence of a transcendent and truly global human identity. I expect that Soka University of America will set a distinguished example in the fulfillment of such a mission and the exposition of such a theme.

As Asia rises and the West declines, it becomes the duty of universities with Asian roots to preserve and further the Western liberal arts tradition. Please hold this duty sacred, so that "the best which has been thought and said" will not be purged from your curriculum, will not be banished from the light of human consciousness, and will stand as a beacon that illuminates inquiring minds. That is the best advice I can offer.

Universities have a big mission to accomplish. The greatest pride of The City College of New York is its mission: to educate the whole people—meaning children of immigrants and others who can't afford Ivy League tuitions but who nonetheless merit opportunities for higher education. City College was known as the "Harvard of the Proletariat." It currently numbers nine Nobel laureates among its distinguished alumni, more than any other public institution in the United States.

IKEDA: What a brilliant tradition! My idea in founding universities is similar: I've often said that "universities should exist for the sake of those who were unable to attend them." While undeniably performing great services for humanity, institutions of higher learning have often been criticized as ivory towers, where people shut themselves away to conduct research divorced from ordinary life. In their rush to cultivate people with the ability to meet society's immediate practical needs, they have sometimes failed to value and foster humane values.

Many leaders, who ought to be working for the good of society and the people, are blighted by an arrogant elitism and motivated by a corrosive drive for personal gain and lust for power. Nichiren decries such people as "talented animals."[14] We must not let our universities produce such individuals. I have consistently stressed the need for institutions of higher learning to cultivate the fully realized individual.

Universities should be producing individuals of intelligence and creativity. This is the purpose behind studying the wisdom and philosophy that is humanity's intellectual legacy—the liberal arts curriculum. The fully realized individual is not a specialist in one narrow field. He or she possesses broad knowledge, sincerity, a sense of responsibility, and the will to work for the happiness of others. This is the person who stands up courageously to improve society in whatever way he or she can.

MARINOFF: I agree with you wholeheartedly. The current economic crisis into which the world has been plunged resulted precisely from what you call a "corrosive drive for personal gain and lust for power."

For decades, too many educational systems have deconstructed (that is, dismantled) the liberal arts tradition, have failed to imbue their students with humanistic virtues, and instead have inculcated shortsighted ideologies and narrow-minded egoism. The time is ripe for what you aptly term "cultivating the fully realized individual."

Life and Death Are Not Separate

IKEDA: These are words of Dame Esther Gress, a poet laureate of Denmark:

> If you want to change the world
> you must change man
> If you want to change man
> you must make him want to
> If you will make man want to change
> you must change the world
> Do that [1]

Gress, always youthful in spirit and exhibiting an optimistic vision, engaged in spirited discussions with young people.

The news today is often dark and disturbing. That's precisely why we, as individuals, must strive to become like bright suns, shining with the light of hope. We need to bravely take one step forward, then another. We need to encourage one another with robust optimism and keep moving onward to the future. This is the way to transform our world in a major way.

MARINOFF: This verse by Gress is thought provoking. Indeed, as Lao Tzu writes, the "journey of a thousand miles / starts from beneath your feet."[2] The biggest step is always the next one.

The baseball player Yogi Berra is famous for making unintentionally humorous and improbably profound statements. He once said, "When you come to a fork in the road, take it." This reiterates humanity's current predicament and Gress's poem: we must follow the forking road, changing ourselves and the world alike.

IKEDA: Indeed, we should. Famous for its dairy industry and windmills, Denmark is a leader in the development of green energy sources, such as wind power and biomass energy production. In recent years, Denmark has also attracted widespread attention for its top ranking in the happiness index.[3] Among the numerous factors accounting for this, a rich culture, a tradition of lifelong education, and an enduring spirit of mutual assistance all seem to play major roles.

MARINOFF: Having visited Denmark, I experienced firsthand the pervasive well-being that emanates from a healthy body politic. As you say, many factors contribute to the high Danish happiness index. In addition to those you mention, one can also note a relatively small population density, clean air and water, compassionate social democracy, religious tolerance, and love of liberty.

Overall happiness remains high in Denmark, even though a lack of sunlight during winter months tends to increase depression in Nordic climes. Culture can be more powerful than geography. A culture such as Denmark's, which manages to incorporate compassion and unity, cannot fail to engender pervasive happiness.

IKEDA: All of my Danish friends radiate this great cultural power. I'm convinced that the key to enabling humanity to recuperate from the sickness that plagues modern civilization is restoring our inherent human powers. Reviving humanity and revealing its inherent virtue are the driving forces to make the world a better place and should, I believe, be the focus of a philosophy aimed at helping people.

MARINOFF: During the past century or so, a small but vital handful of visionaries for humanity have foreseen that our next major steps as a species will be neither biological nor technological but will entail an evolution (or revolution) in human consciousness. You and I agree that philosophy can and must play a pivotal role in enabling the emergence of a truly global civilization.

VICIOUS CIRCLE TO VIRTUOUS CIRCLE

IKEDA: That's one of the main goals of this dialogue. To further its emergence, we indeed need to overcome our present lack of a guiding philosophy. As the Tiantai school teaches, "One who has fallen to the ground recovers and rises up from the ground."[4] The majority of the many problems we face today are, when all is said and done, caused by the human race. It's reasonable to assume that when we ourselves change, we can find solutions to the problems we've caused.

MARINOFF: It's interesting and also refreshing to hear you couch this issue in terms of will—a faculty central to every human aspiration for betterment, yet one that is sorely neglected of late in the global village.

We need to disseminate two ideas above all. First, the exercise of will is the paramount determining factor in the life direction of every human being and can bring about momentous results if mobilized and sustained in virtuous pathways.

Second, neglect of the will leads to political apathy as well as social atrophy, engendering a vacuum that is too often filled by ideologies, dogmas, and bureaucracies, among other obstructive or oppressive mechanisms of political and social control. In sum, people need to be made aware that their wills are largely untapped and are inexhaustible resources that can be developed and applied to the peaceful resolution of every human problem we face.

IKEDA: I vividly recall how Aurelio Peccei, founder of the Club of Rome, stressed in our dialogue (*Before It Is Too Late*, 1985) that the last frontier humanity must develop is the self. Human will—which we could also call the power or energy of life—must be aimed in the right direction and sublimated into good for the sake of society and humanity.

MARINOFF: Philosophy must become an active presence in people's minds and lives, breaking the vicious circle arising from its absence and installing a virtuous circle in its place. In order for this to happen, we need exemplars such as yourself, who have accomplished amazing goals by persistent exercise of beneficent will power.

IKEDA: The great Danish educator Nikolai Grundtvig argues that more useful than books in helping people live meaningful, fulfilling lives are the heart, the kind ear, and voice of a well-balanced person and the vigor gained from engaging in dialogue with enlightened individuals.

A person's worth and happiness are not determined by money, success, or recognition but by the philosophy that person follows and the good he or she does in life. The power of goodness motivates the individual to face and triumph over adversity and, at the same time, imparts hope to others. This power is the commitment to taking action for the happiness of others, the unyielding power of the human spirit at its best. A sound guiding philosophy and inspiring dialogue are the keys to tapping this power of goodness within people's lives and setting them in the right direction.

MARINOFF: As you previously observed (see Conversation Twelve), these vital qualities were articulated by early Buddhism in the eightfold path. Their daily practice mobilizes inner resources that conduce to the achievement of humanity's greatest potential.

We inhabit a cosmic era of increasing entropy: the universe is expanding and cooling; physical systems are moving from orderly toward more disorderly states. Every being and system expend non-recoverable energy over time—whether we are boiling water or running an organization, every process is less than 100 percent efficient. This tendency toward increasing disorder, or cosmically mandated inefficiency, is called "entropy." Life itself is only a temporary resistance to entropy.

Every breath we draw contains a molecule that was once part of Socrates or Confucius or Shakyamuni. And although the molecules that once formed the bodies of these great sages are scattered far and wide by entropy, their wisdom remains intact. Even though we are powerless to prevent entropic dissolution of the flesh, we human beings have the remarkable capacity to transcend physical entropy by instituting moral order in our lives. Moral order emanates from sentience, or consciousness. Buddhism has plumbed the depths of sentience more than any other philosophy.

THE SEA OF LIFE

IKEDA: In its pursuit of the source of this force for good that can overcome the chaos and destruction in the world, Buddhism delves into the inner depths of human life, our inner universe, and illuminates the deepest levels of our beings.

If I may attempt to briefly summarize a very complex system of ideas, the Mahayana Buddhist philosophical school called the Consciousness Only school posited a theory of eight consciousnesses. A ninth consciousness was later added to this system, and this was the form in which the teaching was accepted by Zhiyi and later also endorsed by Nichiren. This system is an attempt to understand the deepest levels of the human mind through a detailed analysis of the precise operations of our consciousness.

The first five consciousnesses are essentially the perceptions of the five sense organs (eyes, ears, nose, tongue, and body, or sense of touch). The sixth, or mind consciousness, has the function of integrating and interpreting this sense data.

The seventh consciousness (*mano-vijnana*) is where the positive and negative mental states—the latter being the obstructions to enlightenment that we've discussed—reside in a state of potentiality. The eighth consciousness (*alaya-vijnana*) is conceived as being where the effects of our deeds are stored as positive and negative karma.

Zhiyi and Nichiren teach a ninth, fundamentally pure consciousness (*amala-vijnana*) underlying the eighth consciousness. The ninth consciousness is the original Life of the universe within each of us. Also called *the palace of the ninth consciousness*, it is the true entity of Life, or, in Nichiren Buddhism, Nam-myoho-renge-kyo.

MARINOFF: This is a comprehensive theory of consciousness, which holds considerable fascination for Westerners, especially in contrast to some of the West's more impoverished and incomplete models of mind. Western philosophers are of course divided on the issues of life, death, and consciousness. Plato believed in the transmigration of the soul (in Greek, *metempsychosis*), an idea he inherited from Pythagoras, who may well have acquired it from Indian philosophy. Bertrand Russell, a classic twentieth-century materialist and atheist, insisted that death is a state of complete dissolution and oblivion—the extinction of being and consciousness.

Epicurus famously says of death, "So long as we exist, death is not with us; but when death comes, then we do not exist."[5] In other words, he believed that it is impossible to experience one's nonexistence from an extant state, just as it is impossible to experience one's existence from a nonextant state.

So the experience of death remains unknowable to us. We witness it concretely when it befalls others but can contemplate it only abstractly in our own cases. How does your Buddhist philosophy approach the idea of death?

IKEDA: Nichiren Buddhism is neither a form of materialism nor immaterialism. It teaches that Life is eternal. Toda often used to say that "after death, our lives merge with the universe." In other words, the cosmos is a great sea of Life, constantly changing as it moves in a ceaseless rhythm of birth and death. The individual life rises as what might be likened to a wave on the surface of that sea, only to subside back into the sea of Life again in death. This rhythm always repeats.

In the Lotus Sutra chapter "The Life Span of the Thus Come One," the Buddha says, "As an expedient means I appear to enter nirvana."[6] The Buddha is saying that he seems to die—"enter nirvana"—in order to motivate living beings to actively pursue their enlightenment without relying on him. In fact, however, the Buddha exists eternally, not as an individual but as the principle of enlightenment.

This can also be interpreted as elucidating the nature of our lives and deaths as individuals. We seem to die—and indeed, as individuals, we do—but we, too, exist eternally, as the principle of Life. The cycle of life and death on the individual level can be likened to the cycle of day and night. Birth is like waking from sleep in the morning; our life is our day's activities; after the workday, weary, we lie down to rest, in death. Buddhism teaches that universal Life, repeating this cycle of individual births and deaths eternally throughout the three existences of past, present, and future, is the true reality of Life.

MARINOFF: Modern physics reveals that matter and energy are neither created nor destroyed; rather, they are conserved. Matter and energy undergo endless transformations in their cyclical propagation through space and time, manifesting here in one form and there in another. Yet nothing is ever lost; in principle, all is accounted for.

This must hold equally true of the vital energy that we call Life and of the sentient radiant energy that we call consciousness. They, too, are conserved. Nothing is ever lost; it is merely transformed. Physics studies laws that govern transformations of matter and energy; Buddhism studies laws that govern transformations of sentient life and consciousness.

WHAT IS DEATH?

IKEDA: Martin Luther King Jr. says, "There is an amazing democracy about death."[7] Everyone dies. In this solemn reality, all people are equal. Pondering our common mortality can help us to transcend our differences and better communicate with one another.

In 2008, the Boston Research Center for the 21st Century (renamed the Ikeda Center for Peace, Learning, and Dialogue in 2009) initiated a series of events on the theme "Understanding Death, Appreciating Life." Among the events held on the theme that year, a seminar on views of death in different civilizations, attended by leading Harvard scholars, was particularly stimulating and aroused great interest.[8] Dialogues of this kind resemble tiny seeds, blooming and bearing fruit with time. They contribute to a new civilization and philosophy.

MARINOFF: Death compels us to reflect on life. I always ask my philosophy students, "What is the leading cause of death?" After they offer the usual answers (e.g., stress, cancer, heart disease), I tell them, "The leading cause of death is birth: it is, sooner or later, 100 percent fatal." At first they laugh, but then their minds open to deeper questions about life and death.

Having visited the Ikeda Center and read many of its fine publications, I highly commend the work that Masao Yokota, Richard Yoshimachi, Virginia Benson, and their colleagues have done and are doing to further intercultural dialogue.

IKEDA: Intercultural dialogue is indeed the very thing we need today. During that February 2008 seminar with Harvard scholars, the Turkish-born cultural anthropologist Nur Yalman said that a culture's view of life and death is an expression of the wisdom of the religions that make up that culture's core belief system. As such, he continued, reconsideration of a culture's views of life and death is a primary method for revitalizing the culture. I believe this to be true and that investigation into the meaning of life and death can provide considerable illumination to a thoroughgoing consideration of the nature of our world today.

MARINOFF: Dr. Yalman is quite correct that each civilization is defined and shaped by its core religions. This was as true of the ancient world as it is of our contemporary one. Moreover, religions that neglect to reexamine their views also fail to evolve and so detract from the longevity of the civilizations they otherwise help sustain. Today's so-called clash of civilizations is at bottom a contest of ideologies, fueled by conflicting religious (and irreligious) views of life and death.

IKEDA: As I suggested in my lecture at Harvard University in 1993, the fact that modern civilization has tried to deny the reality of death and banish it from our awareness has in effect enabled death to loom over us, appearing more menacing than it is. Nichiren Buddhism, however, adopts a view of life and death based on the principle of the arising and extinction of the Dharma nature. In that lecture, I tried to explicate these rather complex Buddhist ideas: the Dharma nature is a name for eternal truth—the true reality of the universe itself. In terms of individual living organisms, the Dharma nature arises as the organism's life and subsides as the organism's death.

No matter how contemporary humanity, under the thrall of desire and other obstructions to enlightenment, tries to ignore the reality of death, it is as much an aspect of existence as is life. There is no escaping its reality.

What is death? Without seriously considering this question, we cannot know what life is either; we lose sight of the true worth and dignity of life, our conscience, and the possibility of living a good, vigorous life. This makes a meaningful, fulfilling life impossible.

The essayist Michel de Montaigne, whose works I loved as a young man, writes:

> That is why all the other actions of our life must be tried and tested by this last act. It is the master day, the day that is judge of all others. "It is the day," says one of the ancients [Seneca], "that must judge all my past years."[9]

PREPARATION FOR A NEW CYCLE

MARINOFF: Without a sound philosophy of life, people may fear death, and their fear will diminish their capacity to live to the fullest. The great British poet John Donne wrote a celebrated poem titled "Death Be Not Proud," in which he espoused the view that, by overcoming our dread of death, we compel death itself to die. Donne used to "practice" being dead: he kept a coffin in his living room and every evening would change into his finest clothes and lie down in it. While such behavior is not atypical of the endearing eccentricities that characterize British culture, it represents a sincere attempt by a Westerner to confront death on a daily basis, so as to better appreciate life.

IKEDA: Many have suggested that modern civilization is so obsessed with life that it tends to forget about or avert its gaze from death. Only through a good life led by directly confronting the reality of death, however, can we make our time here on earth fulfilling and worthwhile. This should be the aim of religious faith and practice.

As I pointed out earlier, the Lotus Sutra teaches the doctrine that, as an expedient means, the Buddha appears to enter nirvana. According to this view, death is a kind of preparation for a new life, for a new cycle of activity. Buddhism offers a true view of life that helps us to meet death without needless fear.

Overcoming the sufferings entailed in birth, aging, illness, and death—the inexorable realities of human existence—was Shakyamuni's main motivation in leaving the secular world and embarking on his quest for truth. Starting from the resolution of the issue of birth and death on the individual level, Shakyamuni revealed the path to overcoming all types of suffering, to relieving the misery and suffering of society and the human race as a whole.

MARINOFF: I share your concerns about technocratic attempts to avoid confronting death. American mass media epitomize this dichotomy. On the one hand, every conceivable violent death is glorified on television, in movies, and via videogames, promoting a culture of neo-Roman circuses and, inevitably, of necrophilia.

On the other hand, people seem completely unequipped to deal with death and dying in real terms when it befalls them or their loved ones. Those who cannot confront death impoverish their experience of life.

IKEDA: This also troubled Toynbee. In our dialogue, we candidly discussed the issues of the worth and dignity of life and the meaning of life and death. When he was young, Toynbee lost many friends in World War I. He kept their photographs on the mantelpiece in his London apartment as treasured mementos, and he felt a deep, abiding indignation that these young men, with their future ahead of them, were robbed of their precious lives by the folly of war.

He said that many leaders in today's society, which is focused exclusively on the pursuit of ephemeral honor and glory, refuse to consider the fundamental reality of life and death. They then cause great unhappiness, he perceptively observed, because without an understanding of the real nature of life and death, they can never create a truly humane civilization.

MARINOFF: As a lifelong devotee of Chinese philosophy, Toynbee was well aware of Confucius's observation that the world's problems will not be solved until sovereigns govern by moral force instead of physical coercion. Of twenty-two great civilizations charted by Toynbee in his magnum opus, *A Study of History*, only three survive today. In his view, the others perished of moral degeneracy.

Coercive forms of government foment needless suffering and engender violent death. The twentieth century sadly witnessed the most devastating examples of such tragic occurrences in human history to date.

KING ASHOKA'S WISE LEADERSHIP

IKEDA: Nothing inflicts more misery on the people of the world than having fools as leaders. We must not allow ourselves to repeat the mistakes that drenched the twentieth century in blood.

I spoke with Toynbee about some of the great leaders in history, including King Ashoka of ancient India. Deeply regretting the terrible loss of life in a war that he himself had started, Ashoka reflected on and repented his actions, turning to Buddhism for solace and guidance. He decided to rule not by force of arms but through the Dharma, or Law, and he created an era of peace. In other words, instead of military might, he exercised great spiritual and moral might to bring peace and stability to society.

In concrete terms, Ashoka based his governance on the principle of the worth and dignity of life, instituting policies embodying this principle, such as renouncing war, guaranteeing his subjects the right to a fair and just trial, and many other critical reforms. He also sent emissaries to neighboring countries to promote regional peace.

In addition, he implemented new social and environmental policies—for example, elevating the status of women and planting shade trees along the realm's roads and byways—and supported cultural activities that stand as a record of achievement deserving our admiration to this day.

A large number of the intellectuals with whom I have talked, including Coudenhove-Kalergi, agree in their high evaluations of King Ashoka.

MARINOFF: Enlightened sovereigns have been relatively few and far between in human history, which is one reason why Ashoka is still venerated today, even in the West. It's difficult indeed to resist corruptions of absolute power. One way is to remain open-minded and willing to learn, which requires humility—a trait too often lacking in high political office.

Marcus Aurelius remained humble: he learned Stoicism from the freed slave Epictetus, thus tempering his power with virtue. He and Ashoka were embodiments of Plato's ideal philosopher-king. A commitment to lifelong learning is surely a key to engendering enlightened sovereigns.

IKEDA: Remaining open-minded and willing to learn are extremely important traits. It is significant that Ashoka was not always the great leader he became. He fundamentally reexamined his way of life after witnessing the brutal slaughter and immense destruction caused by war. By studying the teachings of Buddhism in greater depth, he built a citadel of peace within his heart and then consciously expanded it into the world outside.

I believe that the wisdom of Buddhism can play a major role in creating a peaceful society today, too. In our dialogue (*The Persistence of Religion*, 2009), Dr. Harvey Cox, a leading religious scholar at Harvard, expressed his hope that Buddhism could build a bridge between the Christian and Islamic civilizations.[10]

MARINOFF: I strongly agree with Cox. There are more than three billion Christians and Muslims on this planet. By replicating manyfold the experience shared with me by one of my Muslim students (see Conversation Eight), Buddhism can play a decisive role in transforming inter- and intra-civilizational warfare into global humanism.

Buddhism rejects violence as unworkable, teaching instead the art and science of moral self-government. It enables its practitioners to lead lives of exemplary dignity and quality, and to encourage others to do the same. Buddhism is non-threatening and in fact can enhance the religious experiences of practitioners of other faiths. This applies to Christians and Muslims, as well as to women and men in all walks of life.

By the way, since women live on average longer than men, women must confront the deaths of their loved ones more frequently than men.

IKEDA: That's just the sort of sympathetic insight I have come to expect from you.

In the early Buddhist scripture called the Therigatha (the Pali title of *Verses of the Elder Nuns*), we find numerous stories about female disciples of Shakyamuni who conquered their hardships and sufferings. One story tells of Kisa Gotami, who lost her child. Born into a poor family, the thin, malnourished woman was called Kisa, meaning "skinny." Eventually, she married and gave birth to a son. She loved the infant dearly, but he died. Grief-stricken, cradling the dead child in her arms, she walked through town in search of medicine that could restore him to life. Taking pity on her, Shakyamuni told her that her child would be restored to life if she would bring him a poppy seed from a household where no one had ever died. Following his instructions, Kisa searched the town, asking at every door—but alas, there was no household in which no one had ever died. Finally, she realized that no one can escape death.

Shakyamuni wished to help her realize this truth as a way of healing her grief. Awakening to this reality of human existence, Kisa became a follower of the Buddha and practiced his teachings, inspired, as it were, by the death of her beloved child.

Not even the richest and mightiest can avoid the inevitability of death. The mathematician and philosopher Blaise Pascal writes: "We shall die alone. We must act then as if we were alone. If that were so, would we build superb houses, etc.? We should unhesitatingly look for the truth."[11] Thus, we need to base our lives, I believe, on a profound understanding of our ephemerality.

MARINOFF: You have spoken of the loss of your brother during World War II (see Conversation Two). One of my uncles perished in that war. Death claimed my father when I was fifteen and has also claimed both of my brothers, one in infancy, the other in his thirties. It has sent me reminders, too. Anyone who has experienced a brush with death can feel its imminent and almost palpable presence.

IKEDA: After the war, I learned of my oldest brother's death in battle. In those days, I suffered from tuberculosis. My condition was so serious that doctors predicted I wouldn't live to the age of thirty. My youth during those war years was spent under the constant shadow of death.

After the war, I often talked with my friends about life and mortality. My feelings were reflected in verses from "Morigasaki Beach," a poem I wrote at that time:

> But my friend stands silent
> What way should I choose,
> that my life may wing away
> to far-off gardens of the moon?
> He wipes away the tears, sighing
> My friend in lonely sorrow
>
> I too
> but with one boundless aspiration:
> Make a promise with me
> We'll face life
> whatever pain it brings!
> My friend smiles
> "I'll go along with that!"[12]

It was at this period in my life that I began confronting the fundamental issue of how I ought to live my life. "What is the right way to live?" This was the question I asked my mentor on first meeting him.

He answered with a clear explanation of the purpose of Buddhist faith and practice:

> How can we solve the ultimate question of life and death? This is the hardest problem of all, wouldn't you say? Buddhism calls it the problem of the four sufferings: birth, old

age, sickness and death. Until you can solve it, you cannot find a correct way of life.[13]

At the time, I was skeptical about religion. But after meeting my mentor, who had been imprisoned for opposing militarism based on his Buddhist convictions, I intuitively knew I could trust him.

JOY IN BOTH LIFE AND DEATH

MARINOFF: Buddhist philosophy and practice offer wholesome ways of confronting death and thus of enhancing our appreciation of life.

Paulo Coelho, whose books sell by the millions in dozens of countries, escaped a particularly violent, life-threatening incident during his youth. In recounting the details to me one evening, he said that ever since that day, death has been his constant companion, always walking by his side. And precisely because he keeps daily company with death, he has been able to live as fully as possible.

I'm convinced that people can live as fully as possible only by confronting the issue of death on a daily basis. For example, on awakening each morning, I ask myself, "If this were my last day of life, what would I strive to accomplish today?" Similarly, every night before retiring, I want to be able to say, "Tonight I can fall asleep without regret and not be concerned if I should fail to wake tomorrow because I have done everything that could be done today."

IKEDA: Your words provide much food for thought. Life and death are not separate. By confronting the unavoidable reality of death, we awaken to our own mortality. When we move past that toward the dimension of the eternal, the original, the Life of the universe, we acquire a more substantive view of the life and death of the individual, of human existence, and can make our time here on earth fulfilling, without regrets.

This is the aim of Buddhism, the true aim of religious faith and practice. Leo Tolstoy writes, "Living is joyous, and death, too, is joyous."[14]

Nichiren Buddhism offers a penetrating view of life and death based on its teaching that Life unfolds together with the universe in an eternal cycle of birth and death. This enables us to take equal delight in both its phases, rejoicing in both life and death alike.[15] We can make our existence joyous by firmly establishing within the core of our individual lives a sound view of Life, of life and death.

This is, I believe, an important key to the creation of and advancement toward a new civilization for humanity. As Romain Rolland says, new life emerges from death, and life is eternal. The movement for human revolution that we are practicing on a daily basis in the Soka Gakkai International is a philosophical movement directly linked to a view of life and death that leads to a joyous existence.

MARINOFF: Bringing joy to human life is a fitting note on which to close this conversation on life and death.

My favorite composer, Bach, wrote his most celebrated solo piece, his *Chaconne*, in the aftermath of the sudden death of his beloved young wife, Barbara. In this *Chaconne*, recorded by many virtuoso violinists and guitarists of the twentieth century, Bach explores the depths of his grief to an unprecedented musical extent. The composition leads him—and performers and audiences alike—through a dance of transformation, which begins in despair, leads to serenity, transcends sorrow and joy alike, and culminates in an experience of timeless sanctity.

Your favorite composer, Beethoven, expressed his immortal

"Ode to Joy" in his last and greatest symphony, his ninth. Overcoming his personal impediment of deafness, in addition to the civilizational carnage wrought by the Napoleonic wars, Beethoven transformed his tortured life into triumphant musical gifts of joy for humanity and posterity.

Women and the Building of Peace Cultures

IKEDA: The cheerful voices of women echo with the sound of progress. Their vigorous teamwork brings the light of peace. Recent Soka Gakkai peace-culture forums and exhibitions such as *Women and the Culture of Peace* and *Children and a Culture of Peace* have stimulated great interest throughout Japan.

MARINOFF: I'm well aware of these wonderful undertakings on the part of Soka Gakkai women. In 2008, at the SGI-USA New York Culture Center, I was honored to participate in the Culture of Peace Distinguished Speakers Lecture Series ably organized by Paula Miksic.

IKEDA: These events I mention were organized by Soka Gakkai women to coincide with the UN International Year for the Culture of Peace (2000) and the International Decade for a Culture of Peace and Non-violence for the Children of the World (2001–10).

The surest and most effective way to make the world a better place—for peace and the dignity of life—is to take practical steps in the here and now, sowing and nurturing the seeds for a new culture of peace in our communities and in the lives of those with whom we come into daily contact. These inspiring discussions and efforts at friendly outreach by women are now blossoming beautifully in their communities. Women are seekers of peace philosophies and creators of peace cultures.

MARINOFF: Having met many women involved with the SGI-USA, I'm deeply impressed by their sincere devotion, resolute action, and clear vision for a global culture of peace. Great strides have been made during recent decades toward improving the general condition of women. Even greater progress will follow on the heels of ongoing globalization.

IKEDA: The first step in making the twenty-first a century of peace and respect for the worth and dignity of life is making it the century of women. The action of large numbers of ordinary women awakened to a sense of their global citizenship is absolutely essential. The efforts of women have played a large part in the Soka Gakkai International's movement for peace, culture, and education based on the teachings of Buddhism.

Many of the world's intellectuals with whom I have spoken have stressed that women are the key to the future. In this conversation, let's discuss the activities of women as the focal point of a new age.

MARINOFF: It's certainly fitting for us to explore the role of women in this new millennium.

IKEDA: The futurologist Hazel Henderson, with whom I shared a dialogue (*Planetary Citizenship*, 2004), once said in an interview for the *Seikyo Shimbun* that women have the ability, whether innate or acquired, to see the whole picture and adopt an unbiased viewpoint.

In your philosophical counseling, what especially admirable characteristics have you noticed in women?

MARINOFF: Over the years, I have learned many things from my female clients. A primary lesson is that women tend to pay much more attention to relationships than do men. Men are more objective by nature, tending to objectify and externalize people, things, and processes. Objectivity can further one's non-judgmentalness (and therefore can reduce suffering) but can also dehumanize others, leading to what Martin Buber called unwholesome "I-It" relations.[1]

Women are by nature more subjective, tending to subjectify and internalize relationships. Subjectivity can further one's attachments (therefore potentiating suffering) but can also humanize others, leading to what Buber called wholesome "I-Thou" relations.[2] There's no question that most women value interpersonal relationships above all else.

DIFFERENCES BETWEEN MEN AND WOMEN

IKEDA: Xie Bingxin, a leading Chinese literary figure with whom we were friends, once told my wife and me that if there were no women in the world, society would lose 50 percent of its truth, 60 percent of its goodness, and 70 percent of its beauty. Personally, I think she underestimated.

What's the reason for such differences between women and men? The processes by which they emerge have been studied from a variety of perspectives. Professor Simon Baron-Cohen of Cambridge University, whose research on the differences between men and women has attracted much attention, identifies greater empathy as a special characteristic of women.

He defines empathy as follows:

> Empathizing is about spontaneously and naturally tuning into the other person's thoughts and feelings, whatever these might be. . . . it is about reading the emotional atmosphere between people. It is about effortlessly putting

yourself into another's shoes, sensitively negotiating an interaction with another person so as not to hurt or offend
them in any way, caring about another's feelings.[3]

Women's superiority in language skills has long been recognized. This in combination with their ability to empathize probably makes women better communicators.

MARINOFF: If we wish to learn about processes that give rise to
these and other differences, we must take into account fourteen
million years of primate evolution, which contain the seeds of human behavior. In addition to primatology, we must also study the
physical and cultural anthropology of early hominids through to
our Neanderthal forebears, a period of around four million years. It
turns out that many social consequences of human sex difference
are rooted in biology and cannot be dismissed by wishful thinking,
social engineering, or political indoctrination.

A fundamental fallacy has permeated Western civilization but
not yet Asia: namely, the transparently false proposition that all
differences between men and women are "socially constructed."
People must learn that equality does not entail sameness. One plus
four equals two plus three, but the two formulas are not the same.
I enjoy apples and oranges equally, but they are not the same. We
should love all our children equally, but they are not the same. Yin
and yang are equal in their complementarity, but they are mani-
festly not the same.

Similarly, granting women equal rights and opportunities does
not mean that women will become the same as men. Nor do most
women wish to be. Qualities such as empathy make women invaluable as facilitators of dialogue and as peacemakers. Men often adopt
a confrontational stance, which inhibits communication and can
escalate into conflict. Women often adopt an empathetic stance,
which furthers communication and defuses conflict. Whereas men

are often preoccupied with abstract associations of ideas, women tend to focus on concrete interpersonal relations within the family, the workplace, and the community. They weave and mend familial and social fabrics, upon which so much of our well-being depends.

Female clients have obliged me to explore more attentively those philosophical resources—both Western and Asian—that address themselves to latent and emergent problems in human relationships.

Ikeda: Women indeed strengthen and facilitate the interpersonal bonds that are the bedrock of our societies.

Dr. Baron-Cohen noted that the power of empathy suppresses human aggressiveness, while its absence causes it to increase. Violence is the ultimate result of the absence of empathy. Men often use power to force things through; women, with their greater empathy, tend to pay attention to other people's feelings and circumstances, which makes them better at maintaining harmony. The tendency is of course relative, but for us today, living in a society in which human relations have grown increasingly distant and weak, the ability to empathize is certain to become more and more important for both men and women.

Women As Promoters of Culture

Marinoff: One outstanding female trait, which I have observed continuously in high-energy business arenas, is women's emphasis on the importance of culture. Left to their own devices, many men would devote hour upon hour to business, politics, and sports, to the exclusion of all else. Their wives, on the other hand, would eventually insist that they attend, and be attentive to, cultural events involving music, poetry, literature, painting, or theatre.

Although a good many men are superb performers or creative artists, women above all are the culture-makers—providing the essential social matrix that allows culture to be publicly shared. So women can greatly improve society by continuing further celebrations and refinements of culture. Since cultural expression and appreciation are universal, it is women who socialize and civilize us all, largely through their tireless promotion of culture.

IKEDA: A very important point. Women are without a doubt great creators of the culture of peace. Men need to humbly recognize this and appreciate women's unique contributions.

In our dialogue, Coudenhove-Kalergi, while stressing his belief that world peace can be achieved if we give women the chance to play a bigger role, goes on to draw an interesting comparison. Although little girls all over the world play with dolls, he says, little boys everywhere play at war and are interested in defeating others.

I once heard about an experiment investigating different behaviors in males and females. A group of kindergarten children were segregated by sex. Both groups were given building blocks to play with. In most cases, the boys formed two opposing groups trying to capture each other's blocks, starting a war game. The girls, on the other hand, usually began to talk with one another about what they wanted to build as a group. Of course, this is not how all boys and girls are, but I think it tells us something about male and female tendencies in general.

MARINOFF: Yes, it does. Sex differences in human children have been extensively studied, often by women themselves. There's a huge corpus of objective evidence on the social consequences of sex difference. On average, female children excel in verbal ability; males, in visual-spatial analysis. Females tend to be cooperative and conforming; males, aggressive and competitive. Play groups are largely sex-segregated, but a few girls are found in the largest boys' play groups. Boys are rated as physically tougher than girls as early as nursery-school age, though there's some overlap, with the toughest girls being tougher than the least tough boys. There are dominance hierarchies for both sexes, but the boys' hierarchy tends to be more stable (that is, more agreed upon) than the girls' hierarchy.[4]

Those who teach that girls and boys behave differently solely because of "social construction" of so-called gender roles are sadly deluded. Such radical ideologues have politicized sex difference and in so doing have caused incalculable cultural damage and engendered needless agitation and pointless suffering—among girls, boys, women, and men alike.

To reiterate: these differences stem from fourteen million years of primate evolution. Girls play with dolls and engage in cooperative behaviors because they are rehearsing their evolutionary roles as mothers and socializers; boys play at war and engage in competitive behaviors because they are rehearsing their evolutionary roles as hunters and protectors. For at least two hundred thousand years of human evolution, these natural traits served to further our survival and dispersion across the planet in small hunting and gathering bands that gradually coalesced into tribes and eventually into civilizations. But the corollary cost of this *modus vivendi* has been unremitting conflict and violence on ever-increasing scales.

Culture has the power to override our most dangerous traits or at least to channel them into relatively harmless pursuits such as sports, which William James called the "moral equivalent of war."[5] But the perennial question remains: How can a culture devoted to peaceful pursuits protect or defend itself against a neighboring culture devoted to military conquest?

War Into Peace

Ikeda: As you point out, humanity hasn't yet found a way to overcome this deeply ingrained, thorny problem. It's no exaggeration to say that the steady march of warfare that continued through the twentieth century is a history created by men with their aggressive instincts. Male-dominated society has been characterized by cultures of power, war, and competition.

As Gandhi, in whose nonviolence movement many women participated, writes, "If by strength is meant moral power, then woman is immeasurably man's superior . . . . If nonviolence is the law of our being, the future is with woman."[6] It's crucial to increase our respect for and strengthen the power of women if we are to transform a culture of war into a culture of peace.

MARINOFF: Of course, I agree with you and Gandhi, at least in certain contexts. The most violent criminals and depraved mass murderers are invariably men. Most women can be entrusted with children, whereas many men cannot.

At the same time, not all men are devils, and not all women are angels. Male-dominated societies also produced the Italian Renaissance, the high Baroque, the scientific revolution, the European Enlightenment, the US Declaration of Independence, and the Solvay Conferences, among other lofty pinnacles of cultural achievement.

World-famous anthropologist Margaret Mead warned that if women were divorced from hearth and home, their demonic powers would be unleashed, and they could become even more ruthless and violent than men.[7] Her prediction was borne out during the 1970s and 1980s, when urban guerilla gangs terrorized Western Europe: sixteen of twenty-two "most wanted" terrorists at that time were women. Similarly, during the Vietnam War, US Admiral Elmo Zumwalt observed that the Viet-Cong women were more vicious fighters than the men.[8] And let us be mindful that Adolf Hitler was encouraged by his companion Eva Braun, while Mao Zedong's wife Jiang Qing instigated China's Cultural Revolution, which devastated the Chinese intelligentsia, along with tens of millions of lives.[9]

So we must recognize the overarching importance of social and political norms and women's superior ability to conform to them. Where norms are pacific, women will have the greatest effect in creating and preserving a culture of peace.

IKEDA: All theories about the differences between men and women are generalizations, of course, and there are many exceptions. The important thing is to discover ways to tap and make good use of women's outstanding traits while transforming male-dominated society into one in which the sexes are balanced and harmonized. The key to achieving this is for a philosophy of peace, a philosophy of the worth and dignity of life, to serve as the foundation for society.

I know countless women, all of them ordinary citizens, who have, based on their Buddhist beliefs, contributed on a daily basis to the welfare of others and society for the sake of creating a culture of peace. I've occasionally composed poetry to encourage and support them.

For example:

You are all
youthful Buddhas
striving wholeheartedly
day after day,
no matter how busy
or how tired you are,
for the happiness of your friends
who are suffering
or in sorrow . . . .

With sincerity,
you rush to the aid
of others.

You go out of your way
to find and help
those who are struggling.
And how beautiful is
the heart-to-heart support
and encouragement
you give one another!

What an example
of genuine nobility you are!
In today's hectic world,
how precious is your existence![10]

These women's lives are filled with courage, caring, and respect for human beings. Their altruistic actions—transforming their lives and cheerfully, vibrantly striving to help others and lead them to happiness—are a steady source of light in an age lacking a guiding philosophy.

In his *Treatise on the Great Perfection of Wisdom*, Nagarjuna speaks of the four infinite virtues: boundless pity, boundless compassion, boundless joy, and boundless impartiality. These are four boundless forms of the spirit to help others. Pity is true friendship and affection. Compassion is the caring mind that eliminates the sufferings of sentient beings and brings them happiness. Nagarjuna interprets pity as corresponding to imparting delight or happiness to living beings and compassion as eliminating suffering.

The infinite virtue of boundless joy means freeing others from suffering and bringing forth their joy. Impartiality is the spirit of treating people equally, seeing beyond their differences.

The bodhisattva is defined in Buddhism as a being who dedicates his or her life to the welfare of others based on this spirit of true love and concern. This bodhisattva engages in this practice of eliminating suffering and imparting joy, struggling resolutely against evils and injustices that harm people. Buddhism teaches that a life embodying these four infinite virtues is the way to create a true culture of peace.

VISIONARY WOMEN

MARINOFF: It's clear to modern scholars that women excel in caring for others.[11] This would suggest that women are ideally suited to Nagarjuna's *Treatise on the Great Perfection of Wisdom*.

The ancient Greeks were well aware of the power of virtue in women. Aristophanes wrote a satirical play called *Lysistrata*, in which women attempted to establish peace by withholding sexual favors from men until the men disarmed themselves and ceased fighting. This strategy, appealing to vice instead of virtue, didn't succeed.

Antigone, the heroine of Sophocles' famous play, epitomizes the triumph of virtue itself. And let us remember that Plato envisioned women and men sharing political power equally, as virtuous Guardians of his utopian *Republic*.

Even so, it seems to me that Buddhism has more thoroughly and universally articulated the theory and practice of virtue as a force for peace. Now that women are becoming more liberated and empowered, we can see empirically that their virtues are manifest in every field of human endeavor. Women have become great contributors to social reform, justice, and humanistic global civilization.

IKEDA: I've had opportunities to talk with a number of unforgettable women leaders and intellectuals, including Madam Deng Yingchao, who, with Premier Zhou Enlai, helped build the new China; the civil rights leader Rosa Parks; the first female cosmonaut, Valentina Tereshkova; Nobel peace laureate Wangari Maathai; president of the World Centers of Compassion for Children International, Betty Williams; celebrated art historian Axinia Djourova; and many others.

All of them impressed me as warmly compassionate, tolerant individuals while at the same time people of remarkable courage and intelligence, determined opponents of all threats to human worth and dignity. The same wisdom, sense of justice, refusal to compromise with evil, determination to fight for what's right, and inexhaustible perseverance are found in the women of the Soka Gakkai International and have made the organization what it is today, for which I'm deeply grateful.

MARINOFF: Like you, I've been fortunate to encounter many outstanding women who've played and continue to play pivotal roles in visionary education, organization, leadership, and philosophical practice. For example, I owe debts of profound gratitude to Professor Elaine Newman, founder of Science College at Concordia University in Montreal; Professor Yolanda Moses, former president of The City College of New York; Dr. Vaughana Feary, cofounder of the American Philosophical Practitioners Association; Maria Cattaui, former managing director of the World Economic Forum; and the late Laura Huxley, musician, author, social reformer, and wife of Aldous Huxley. These women have made the world a vastly better place by creating value for others. Each one personally gave me her unstinting encouragement and taught me invaluable lessons I shall remember for life.

MEN, WOMEN, AND THE PATH

IKEDA: I'm touched by your spirit of gratitude.

When Nichiren was persecuted by the authorities and his life was in peril, several nameless women stood by him, with no thought of the risk to their safety. Women, and ordinary citizens in general, can demonstrate tremendous strength at decisive moments.

Nichiren encouraged and praised these women by referring to them as sages and holy persons. Reflecting his deep care and concern for them, most of his surviving letters are written in the phonetic syllabary called *hiragana*, so that those who lacked mastery of the Chinese characters used by the educated classes could understand them.

Mahayana Buddhism teaches the value and equality of all life. Nichiren asks, "Do not these interpretations make clear that, among all the teachings of the Buddha's lifetime, the Lotus Sutra is first, and that, among the teachings of the Lotus Sutra, that of women attaining Buddhahood is first?"[12]

He shared with his female followers the account in the Lotus Sutra of the attainment of Buddhahood by the dragon king's daughter, who symbolizes that all women can attain Buddhahood. The heroine of the story is the eight-year-old daughter of the dragon king—not only is she female, but she also resides in the world of animality. Some suggest she represents those who were discriminated against and oppressed in ancient Indian society, the original context of the sutra. Responding to her teacher Shakyamuni's expression of confidence in her, she boldly announces her enlightenment and calls on the assembly to witness it. As proof of her Buddhahood, she then appears in a glorious form expounding the Mystic Law to all sentient beings.[13]

The Buddhahood of the daughter of the dragon king expresses the idea that all, regardless of gender or ethnicity, possess the infinite potential of the Buddha world within themselves. It is a brilliant drama revealing how we can all develop the supreme nature within ourselves.

MARINOFF: That we all can do so, women and men alike, is indicative of our shared humanity. For although Nature has ordained that our species (among innumerable others) shall manifest in two complementary forms—female and male—they are both manifestations of one thing only: humanity.

Just as yin and yang both spring from Tao, so do women and men of every nation, ethnicity, and culture share a common source: human nature. This is also the wellspring of our limitless possibilities, attainable by all fortunate enough to be born as humans and to strive on the path toward Buddhahood.

IKEDA: Precisely. The dragon king's daughter manifests her Buddhahood—her self in possession of the highest state that exists, the Buddha state of being—as a person who devotes herself entirely to teaching the Law to others. This is an indication that the actions of the bodhisattvas, who also dedicate themselves to helping others, are the manifestation of the Buddha state of being.

The dragon king's daughter's announcement of Buddhahood was indeed a great declaration that compassion and wisdom—igniting the flames of hope and courage in others' hearts and awakening their inner strength to live life to the fullest—are equally present in all living beings.

MARINOFF: Good deeds, kind words, compassionate hearts, and awakened minds are neither male nor female; rather, they are human. Goodness, kindness, compassion, and awakening transcend all differences.

IKEDA: Very true. Exactly. Encouragement of people and acts of caring have nothing to do with social position, wealth, or education. Tremendous potential exists in the life of every individual. Philosophy, education, and religion exist to enable people to demonstrate their fullest humanity, each in their unique way.

To Relieve Suffering and Impart Joy

IKEDA: Travel to new places results in new encounters. New dialogues open new paths.

As a philosopher of action, you've traveled all over the world speaking about philosophy. How many nations have you visited?

MARINOFF: During the past decade, I have made more than five dozen trips to dozens of nations across the Americas and throughout Europe. In the Middle East, I've visited Egypt, Israel, and the United Arab Emirates; in Asia, Australia, China, India, Japan, Singapore, South Korea, Taiwan, and Tibet. I've sent my books to many sub-Saharan Africans who have written to request them, most recently responding to requests from Mauritius, South Africa, and Zimbabwe.

IKEDA: I understand that you recently visited Costa Rica, Cyprus, Sweden, and Spain as well. The great interest in your practical philosophical counseling seems to indicate that many people are eagerly seeking paradigms to guide them and a sustaining purpose and meaning in life.

Precisely because of the political and economic turbulence of our times, philosophical dialogue is all the more important. In an unsettled world, dialogue in which we work together to find wiser ways of living offers a method for all of us to come together and become better people.

I'm sure many places and encounters during your travels have made a strong impression on you. What part of your homeland of Canada do you like best?

MARINOFF: Every country I have visited has beautiful scenery and impressive people. I have wonderful memories of them all. My two visits to Japan to meet with you (2003 and 2007) have been especially memorable.

At home, I favor scenic Atlantic Canada—as do many Japanese people who travel to Prince Edward Island to experience the locales depicted in *Anne of Green Gables*.

IKEDA: In 2008, the centennial anniversary of the publication of *Anne of Green Gables*, many people visited Prince Edward Island. L.M. Montgomery's books, including *Anne of Green Gables*, are very popular with Japanese women. In my speeches to young people, I frequently refer to Anne's brave, cheerful way of life.

Rector Elizabeth R. Epperly of the University of Prince Edward Island is a leading expert on Montgomery. I agree with her that one reason the world depicted in *Anne of Green Gables* is so widely loved and appreciated throughout the world is that it represents a message of hope in the face of adversity. Dr. Epperly also thinks that Anne's story conveys the important message that we should seek our home within our hearts. As Epperly explains it, we all come into the world alone, orphans, as it were; by finding home within ourselves—in other words, our reason for existence—we can establish a strong identity and develop an open heart that allows us to form friendships with all we meet.

In this sense, Anne's story explores how to create an ideal community. The required optimism, openheartedness, and positivity are all important for global citizens, Epperly says. She offers a thought-provoking interpretation of Montgomery's work.

MARINOFF: This is a compelling insight from Epperly. Most of us become orphans, eventually outliving our parents, and most of us come to inhabit several or many places during our lifetimes. Yet our fundamental human quest is to find a spiritual home within and a community without. So perhaps *Anne of Green Gables* is coming of age as a model for global citizenship.

CANADA'S BEAUTY

IKEDA: Growing up should bring fulfillment, joy, and hope. *Anne of Green Gables* is a precious gift from your homeland to eager young minds all over the world.

Let's talk a little more about Canada. In addition to literary treasures of this kind, your homeland has a vast treasury of natural riches.

MARINOFF: In the West, I favor the majestic Rocky Mountains and the geographically exquisite province of British Columbia, with its giant fir trees, rugged Pacific coastline, and English gardens on Vancouver Island. My favorite region of all is my native province of Quebec, whose deciduous forests, undulating hills, meandering rivers, and sparkling lakes were the paradise of my youth. Every spring, their spirit beckons me back.

Have you visited Canada?

IKEDA: Yes, three times. I found Vancouver, Toronto, and Montreal beautiful cities, and I was struck by how Canadians value nature. The scale is so much more vast and imposing than in Japan. And I could never forget Niagara Falls.

What impressed me most, though, was the shining character of my Canadian friends. After delivering my 1993 Harvard lecture, I traveled to Montreal to take part in a meeting of Soka Gakkai International members. I vividly remember how delighted everyone was when a giant rainbow appeared against the beautiful blue sky as the meeting ended.

As a small token of appreciation for my Canadian friends' efforts, I wrote this verse:

> Like a scene from a fairy tale
> painted on the canvas
> of the heavens,
> a magnificent rainbow
> crowns you all with its luminous glow.[1]

Quebec, your home province, is indeed a wonderful place. Both the scenery and the people's hearts are beautiful.

MARINOFF: Canadian scenery is idyllic indeed. I'm glad you have experienced it and that you have also visited Canada's leading cities.

Quebec is nicknamed *La Belle Province*, the Beautiful Province. Its island of Montreal, named after the extinct volcano that created it (Mount Royal, or *Mont Royal* in French), is my hometown. Thanks to its bicultural French and British heritage, Montreal is the most European city of North America.

IKEDA: Yes, I've heard that. In your travels, you've certainly encountered a diverse range of different regions and cultures. In dealing with this regional and cultural diversity, what have you been especially careful of?

MARINOFF: As you say, every nation—every culture—has its own distinct philosophical climate. These climates continue to evolve over time, however slowly. Since philosophy is a journey that usually begins with familiar ideas but often leads to unfamiliar ones, I try to understand the background assumptions and worldviews of each particular region and culture. If we begin philosophizing from a familiar or established departure point, it then becomes easier to introduce new ideas.

So when planting philosophical seeds in different soils, one must naturally take into account the indigenous ethos and traditions. This allows the seeds to germinate and the plants to flower.

THE TASTE OF LIBERATION

IKEDA: That's a perceptive observation. Nichiren writes:

> One should . . . have a correct understanding of the country. People's minds differ according to their land. . . . Even plants and trees, which have no mind, change with their location. How much more, then, must beings with minds differ according to the place![2]

No philosophy can expect to take root if it ignores cultural and ethnic characteristics. Buddhism teaches a principle called, in Japanese, *zuiho bini*, or adapting the rules to match the place. *Zuiho* means "according to the place," and *bini* is part of the word for the Buddhist rules of self-discipline—or by extension, the rules of correct behavior to be observed in life.

In other words, the best way to spread the teachings of Buddhism is to respect the traditions, customs, and manners of the place and time, as long as doing so doesn't violate the basic Buddhist precepts of compassion and wisdom. Respecting and learning from the local traditions and culture facilitate communication and promote mutual understanding. The aim is to adapt to different conditions and cultures, and allow new seeds to germinate, resulting in growth for all involved. Only then does the creation of new values become possible.

You've dealt with many people who are trying to work out problems in their lives. Have you adopted different approaches for different countries and cultures?

MARINOFF: You're making a very important point, which accounts for Buddhism's successful and ongoing transplantation worldwide into many and varied cultural soils and climates. Similarly, in my work, I try to conduct with each and every client a philosophical exploration of his or her particular mindscape. People's worldviews are shaped not only by their locally shared norms and values but also by their individual experiences in life, which are bound to admit unique features. My approach is to center each inquiry in the mind of the inquirer, taking into account that person's background culture and personal views.

Even so and notwithstanding all these differences, we are all human. Thus, the essence of human nature and likewise the essence of human happiness and suffering share a common denominator worldwide, irrespective of culture. Did not Shakyamuni say that the vast oceans have but one taste—the "universal salty taste"? So I have found that, despite all the differences between and among peoples, human suffering also has "one taste" that transcends other distinctions.

Yes, there are distinctive national and cultural ways of reacting to suffering, some of which unfortunately exacerbate the problem. But the Dharma has one taste—the taste of liberation—which happily transcends national and cultural differences.

IKEDA: Human beings are just that, human beings. Buddhism aims to enable all human beings to vanquish the suffering that's common to us all, the pain entailed in birth, aging, illness, and death—and furthermore to break free from the ignorance within life that's the fundamental cause of our misery and unhappiness. Again, Buddhism seeks to relieve suffering and impart joy for all, and these goals know no boundaries or ethnic divisions.

In "On Establishing the Correct Teaching for the Peace of the Land," Nichiren asks, "If you care anything about your personal security, you should first of all pray for order and tranquillity throughout the four quarters of the land, should you not?"[3] If you desire happiness and peace of mind, you must first strive for "order and tranquillity throughout the four quarters of the land"—that is, social stability and world peace. Buddhism teaches that personal happiness and world peace are two sides of the same coin.

The world citizens of the future will need to see things from a global perspective and pray and act for the happiness of both themselves and all others.

MARINOFF: The interconnectedness enabled by globalization highlights Buddhism's basic tenets in new and clarion ways. For example, global media coverage of human suffering in a particular region can stimulate swift and compassionate response from all quarters—as, for example, in the aftermath of the devastating tsunami that inundated South Asia in December 2004.

Conversely, unresolved suffering in one part of the world can have severe repercussions in another part—as the global village learned to its horror on September 11, 2001. Thus, globalization cannot succeed unless it adopts an enlightened view of humanity, like that espoused by Buddhism.

REMOVING THE ARROW

IKEDA: Through today's globalization, human encounters and the exchange of goods and information are taking place at a rapidly accelerating pace, and the ties linking us to one another are being strengthened. Therefore, the important question, as you suggest, is how to expand profound spiritual exchange and promote empathy.

The many issues facing society and the world today are bringing us together in a network of often-imperceptible bonds of common interest. To create a world of peace and symbiosis, we need to strengthen these bonds of mutual interest through spiritual exchange at the deepest level and share one another's joys and sufferings.

Life itself is our most profound, inclusive common ground. Buddhism focuses on and illuminates life.

MARINOFF: For those with access, the Internet and cyberspace transcend political and other traditional boundaries, linking persons and networks in emergent global contexts. No place on earth can be called remote any longer.

I believe that people's everyday experiences may be the most effective teachers of universal identification. As globalization evolves, enabling the dissemination of products and ideas from every culture worldwide, more and more "imperceptible bonds" will not only become visible but also palpable, convincing people of our connectedness.

Like a pebble tossed into a pond, the waves from which propagate in all directions, each person exerts a ripple effect on his or her immediate environs, which likewise propagates throughout the social nexus and indeed the cosmos. As people become more aware of their causal influence on and in this nexus, they will surely choose to exert wholesome rather than deleterious influences.

IKEDA: You're describing what's called *dependent origination* in Buddhism. In *The Middle Way*, you observe that to overcome opposition in the world we must be united on the basis of our shared humanity. I, too, believe that just such a shared foundation as fellow human beings is the starting point for overcoming our differences and forming deep spiritual bonds.

Shakyamuni identified the fixation on our differences, manifesting as things like tribal and national affiliations, as the cause of all human conflict. I think we can call this the underlying spirit of discrimination, dividing people into "me" versus "you," "us" versus "them," and then reifying those abstract distinctions. Shakyamuni says, "I perceived a single, invincible arrow piercing the hearts of the people."[4] This arrow is the obsession with our differences, which is piercing our innermost beings. He insisted that we need to remove this arrow from our hearts.

MARINOFF: The key concept is transcendence. Biologically, humans are one species, but for a long time, natural selection favored human dispersion via competitive and often hostile tribes. Political and religious cultures have the unfortunate tendency of enlarging the totems of tribalism, depicting one's own tribe (e.g., nation or religion) as superior and demeaning other tribes as inferior or subhuman.

By contrast, a real global citizen views all human beings not only as one species biologically but also as one community globally. Only a transcendent philosophy can inculcate this view. Such a philosophy must teach people that cultural diversity produces beautiful human mindscapes, just as geographical diversity produces beautiful natural landscapes. In other words, global citizenship requires a philosophy that respects and values local cultures and also transcends them in order to unify humanity.

ALIGNING HEARTS AND MINDS

IKEDA: That's a very important perspective. Historically, ethnic groups have evolved their own diverse cultures, values, and spiritual traditions of life and death. But when ethnic groups with distinct identities have come into contact with one another, friction and obsession with one another's differences have arisen. The question is how we can overcome these fixations with difference and build a common foundation as fellow human beings.

I've always stressed inner universality as that common foundation. Buddhism teaches an inherent universality existing within all human beings—our equality as human beings and a shared foundation of human dignity. When we base ourselves on that foundation, we can transcend all ethnic, cultural, and religious discrimination and eliminate fixation on our differences.

Nichiren employs the metaphor of the cherry, plum, peach, and damson[5] to make this point. When all of these trees blossom with their distinct forms and unique characters, they form a lovely orchard. Similarly, when individuals exhibit their unique worth and personality in their lives, a harmonious society characterized by the creation of diverse values is constructed.

Globalism and universalism transcend ethnic and national frameworks but tend to do so only superficially, from the outside. One of the deleterious effects of this is that economic globalization is deepening and widening the economic gap between the have and have-not countries and regions. It may also spawn new conflicts by ignoring humanity's shared foundation and creating hierarchies based on superficial, external values and measures.

MARINOFF: Economic globalization has unfortunately given rise to two-tiered scenarios from which some nations and regions derive enormous prosperity, while others fall even further behind. As you say, this is bound to spawn new conflicts. I'm convinced that economic development alone isn't sufficient to knit humanity into a vital whole. In parallel, we must inculcate a corresponding set of transcendent human virtues.

Said another way, globalization may succeed in aligning universal human appetites and in dampening long waves of political and religious conflicts that have inundated innocents in every century. But in tandem with aligning human appetites, we must also align human hearts and minds. Globalization has set the stage for this, but the task itself falls primarily to leaders, educators, and philosophers who can bring out the best in all humanity while discouraging the worst.

RELIGION IN A GLOBAL CIVILIZATION

IKEDA: The true gauge of human cultural progress is surely the extent to which our best inner strengths are tapped and employed for the sake of all people.

In our dialogue, when we discuss relations between civilization and religion, Toynbee says: "I believe that a civilization's style is the expression of its religion. I quite agree that religion has been the source of the vitality that has brought civilizations into being and has then kept them in being."[6] I believe that from this point on, religion must be the source for creating a new global civilization and must draw out our best strengths. As we move into the future, ensuring that religion plays this role will become increasingly important.

MARINOFF: I agree with you and Toynbee regarding such connections. Given that a new civilization must be inclusive and global, in my view, no religion that binds its adherents to external, supernatural godheads can nurture such a civilization. The world has already seen any number of such religions evolve. Although they all claim to be based on universal love, and while exponents of such love can be found among them all, some of the most heinous crimes ever committed against humanity have been enacted in the names of these godheads.

The binding force of a new civilizational religion must be internal and not external. Its philosophical mission must be twofold: first, to help people channel their instinctive capacities for reverence away from abstract external deities and toward the concrete manifestation of each person's innate nobility and greatness; and second, to help craft our social and political institutions so as to nurture that kind of secular, humanistic concern.

IKEDA: The two missions you describe are like the wheels of a two-wheeled cart, and a thriving humanity must serve as the axle connecting them.

Buddhism's gaze is directed inward, where it discovers an inner cosmos in the depths of our lives. In other words, it seeks an inherent universality shared by all human beings. This inner journey moves from the individual to embrace the family, the ethnic group, the country, the human race, and all life on the planet, culminating in an awareness of the fundamental principle of the entire universe.

There is within human beings a wonderful quality that merges with the Life of the universe and partakes of the fundamental Law. This Buddha nature is characterized by a worthiness, a dignity, and a greatness that transcend all external differences; it is a manifestation of the "transcendent human virtues" that you describe. It encompasses the virtues of the Middle Way and the golden ratio, as well as love of humanity and the virtues of compassion, justice, courage—and all the other virtues, too. These virtues give us control over our desires and make harmony possible between the heart and the intellect.

MARINOFF: Although Buddhism arrived relatively recently in the West, significant fragments of its transcendent teachings were anticipated by some of the seminal Western philosophers, including Socrates, Plato, and Aristotle. The ancient Greeks strove to harmonize the three components of the secular soul: the rational mind, the emotive heart, and the desirous instinct. They understood the vital importance of inculcating virtues, without which we are no better than savage beasts. Indeed, whenever civilizations neglect to transcend cosmetic differences, they succumb to divisiveness, injustice, and violence.

Thanks to globalization, it is possible, for the first time in human history, to inculcate truly universal virtues, thus helping humanity align itself with the cosmos. I believe that Buddhism has a key role to play in this process.

IKEDA: How can Mahayana Buddhism contribute to twenty-first-century civilization? In my 1993 Harvard lecture, I summarized its potential in three points: it can serve as a wellspring of peace creation, establish a paradigm for restoring humanity, and provide the basis for the symbiotic coexistence of all things.

What determines whether our civilization flourishes or perishes, finds happiness or suffers in misery, are not only external revolutions and reforms but, most important, an inner revolution—a transformation of our views of Life and of birth and death. This is particularly true in this century.

I believe that Soka Gakkai International members' daily efforts in our movement for human revolution, based on the principle of respect for the worth and dignity of life, can make a major contribution in this regard. The Soka Gakkai International people's movement—starting from the inner transformation of the individual and sending waves of revitalization, harmony, and symbiosis into society and the planet to create a new world civilization—has now spread to 192 nations and territories. I regard it, at the same time, as a philosophical movement restoring to humanity the exalted spirituality and religiosity that are being lost in the deep shadows cast by materialistic civilization.

INNER TRANSFORMATION

MARINOFF: As one who has experienced and witnessed time and again the momentous effects—for better and for worse—of attitudes and beliefs, principles and ideas, on the human condition, I can only stand in awe of your mission, vision, and achievements in the service of human revolution. We can't overemphasize the importance of internal transformation in the realization of peace, prosperity, and symbiosis. You and the Soka Gakkai International deserve enormous credit and merit much gratitude for engendering and fostering this kind of transformation for so many people worldwide.

IKEDA: Thank you for your words of deep understanding. The value of the philosophy of human happiness that you and I have been exploring together is revealed in actions to build a society of symbiosis. Its restoration will amount to a philosophical renaissance.

The philosophy of global citizens must be a philosophy of courageous action based on conviction in and commitment to striving together to exhibit the goodness within all our lives. In it beats a profound heart of compassion. Without courage, that compassion cannot be manifested.

As a philosophical practitioner and as a world citizen, I am determined to keep pressing ahead with you, Dr. Marinoff, to bring about a renaissance of humankind and life. I'm deeply grateful to have had this opportunity to take part in this dialogue with you. Thank you.

MARINOFF: You're more than welcome, President Ikeda. It has been an extraordinary privilege to join in dialogue with you—a soul-searching and life-altering experience. Our interaction has greatly enhanced my philosophical practice and so has brought palpable benefits to others in turn. Many owe you their profound gratitude.

Our wide-ranging explorations of philosophy, Buddhism, and

globalization will, I hope, encourage and inspire readers to re-double their commitment to making this world a better place for all. I reciprocate your unwavering resolve and readiness for our continued collaboration toward a new age of human renaissance.

Selected Works
Daisaku Ikeda

Before It Is Too Late: A Dialogue, with Aurelio Peccei. London: I. B. Tauris & Co., Ltd, 2009 (first published in 1984).

Creating Waldens: An East-West Conversation on the American Renaissance, with Ronald A. Bosco and Joel Myerson. Boston: Dialogue Path Press, 2009.

The Persistence of Religion: Comparative Perspectives on Modern Spirituality, with Harvey G. Cox. London: I. B. Tauris & Col., Ltd., 2009.

A Quest for Global Peace: Rotblat and Ikeda on War, Ethics and the Nuclear Threat, with Joseph Rotblat. London: I.B. Tauris & Co., Ltd., 2007.

Ningen shugi no hata o (Hoisting the Banner of Humanism), with Felix Unger. Tokyo: Institute of Oriental Philosophy, 2007. Available only in Japanese.

ˌbachev and Ikeda on Bud-
ˌris & Co., Ltd., 2005.

ˌ and Actions Can Shape a
ˌderson. Santa Monica, Ca-

ˌe Land of Children) with Albert
ˌ, 1998. Available only in Chinese,

ˌ J. Toynbee. Oxford: Oxford University
ˌblished 1976).

ˌgashi (Civilization, East and West), with Count
ˌoudenhove-Kalergi. Tokyo: Sankei Shimbunsha,
ˌvailable only in Japanese.

ˌr more information, go to http://www.daisakuikeda.org/sub/books/
books-by-category.html.

APPENDIX 2

Selected Works
Lou Marinoff

El Poder del Tao (The Power of Tao). Barcelona, Bogota, Buenos Aires, Mexico City, Miami, Montevideo, Santiago de Chile: Ediciones B, 2011.

The Middle Way: Finding Happiness In a World of Extremes. New York: Sterling, 2007.

The Big Questions: How Philosophy Can Change Your Life. New York: Bloomsbury, 2003.

Philosophical Practice. New York: Elsevier, 2001.

Plato, Not Prozac!: Applying Eternal Wisdom to Everyday Problems. New York: HarperCollins, 1999.

For more information, go to http://www.loumarinoff.com/books.htm.

Notes

Conversation One
Philosophy Begins With Questioning

1. This dialogue was originally serialized in Japanese in *Pumpkin* magazine, June 2008–October 2009.
2. Lou Marinoff, *Plato Not Prozac!: Applying Eternal Wisdom to Everyday Problems* (New York: HarperCollins, 1999).
3. Victor Hugo, *Things Seen* (New York: The Colonial Press Co., 1887), p. 140.
4. Offerings, or almsgiving, is one of the six *paramitas*, the practices required of bodhisattvas in order to attain Buddhahood. (Source: *The Soka Gakkai Dictionary of Buddhism* [Tokyo: Soka Gakkai, 2002], pp. 611–12)
5. Nichiren (1222–82) is the founder of the Buddhist tradition that is based on the Lotus Sutra and urges chanting the phrase *Nam-myoho-renge-kyo* as a daily practice. The Soka Gakkai International is based on Nichiren's teachings. (Source: *The Soka Gakkai Dictionary of Buddhism*, p. 439)
6. Nichiren, *The Record of the Orally Transmitted Teachings*, trans. Burton Watson (Tokyo: Soka Gakkai, 2004), p. 115.
7. *The Writings of Nichiren Daishonin*, vol. I (Tokyo: Soka Gakkai, 1999), p. 302.
8. Ibid., 303.
9. Ibid., 998.
10. Daisaku Ikeda, "Graduation Remarks," *World Tribune*, May 18, 2007, p. 2.
11. Lou Marinoff, *The Big Questions: How Philosophy Can Change Your Life* (New York: Bloomsbury, 2003), p. xii.
12. *The Writings of Nichiren Daishonin*, vol. II (Tokyo: Soka Gakkai, 2006), p. 844.
13. Friedrich Wilhelm Nietzsche, *The Portable Nietzsche*, ed. and trans. Edward Kaufmann (New York: Penguin Books, 1954, 1982), p. 126.
14. Daisaku Ikeda, *Discussions on Youth* (Santa Monica, Calif.: World Tribune Press, 2010), pp. 87–88.

CONVERSATION TWO
GRATITUDE TO OUR PARENTS

1. Lou Marinoff, *The Middle Way: Finding Happiness In a World of Extremes* (New York: Sterling, 2007).
2. *The Rubáiyát of Omar Khayyam: The Astronomer Poet of Persia*, quatrain XXVIII, trans. Edward FitzGerald (Philadelphia: John C. Winston, 1889), p. 34.
3. *The Analects of Confucius*, trans. Burton Watson (New York: Columbia University Press, 2007), p. 50.
4. Mikhail Gorbachev and Daisaku Ikeda, *Moral Lessons of the Twentieth Century* (London: I. B. Tauris, 2005), p. 14.
5. *The Writings of Nichiren Daishonin*, vol. I, p. 931.
6. Ralph Waldo Emerson, "Woman," in *Miscellanies* (Boston: Houghton Mifflin Company, 1878), p. 409.

CONVERSATION THREE
CALLING FORTH THE "INNER PHILOSOPHER"

1. *The Writings of Nichiren Daishonin*, vol. II, p. 87.
2. Soka schools: The Soka Junior and Senior High Schools established by Daisaku Ikeda in Kodaira, Tokyo, in 1968, were the beginning of the Soka school system, which today includes kindergartens, elementary, junior and senior high schools, a university in Japan, and a university in Aliso Viejo, Calif. Kindergartens have also been established in Hong Kong, Singapore, Malaysia, South Korea, and Brazil. The educational system is based on the pedagogy of founding Soka Gakkai president and educator Tsunesaburo Makiguchi, who believed that the focus of education should be the lifelong happiness of the learner. Makiguchi was concerned with the development of the unique personality of each child, and he emphasized the importance of leading a socially contributive life.
3. Julian Lloyd Webber, *Song of the Birds: Sayings, Stories, and Impressions of Pablo Casals* (London: Robsons Books, 1985), p. 85.
4. Gregor Piatigorsky, *Cellist* (Garden City, New York: Doubleday, 1965), pp. 28–29.
5. Helen Keller, *Optimism: An Essay* (New York: C. Y. Crowell and Company, 1903), p. 26.
6. Tsunesaburo Makiguchi (1871–1944) was a forward-thinking educational theorist and religious reformer in Japan. His opposition to Japan's militarism and nationalism led to his imprisonment and death during World War II. Makiguchi is best known for two major works, *The Geography of Human Life* and *The System of Value-Creating Pedagogy*, and as founder, with Josei Toda in 1930, of the Soka Gakkai, which is today the largest lay Buddhist organization in Japan. Through the Soka Gakkai International, it has 12 million members worldwide. Consistent throughout his writing and in his work as a classroom teacher and school principal is his belief in the centrality of the happiness of the individual. This same commitment can be seen in his role as a religious reformer: he rejected the attempts of authorities to subvert the essence of the Buddhist teachings, insisting that religion always exists to serve human needs.
7. Since 2000, Marinoff has worked with world leaders in Davos, as Faculty of

the World Economic Forum; in Geneva, for the WEF's Young Global Leaders; with state legislators and senior civil servants at the University of Arizona's South-West Leadership and Governance Program; with senior civil servants in Mexico and Singapore; with future scientific leaders at BioVision in Lyon and the Festival of Thinkers in Abu Dhabi; and with business leaders from Arabia, China, India, and Russia with Horasis in Zurich.

8. Daisaku Ikeda, *The New Human Revolution*, vol. 3 (Santa Monica, Calif.: World Tribune Press, 1996), p. 92.

CONVERSATION FOUR
THE SOURCE OF ROBUST OPTIMISM

1. September 2001 *Art of Living* [SGI-UK], p. 19.
2. *The Writings of Nichiren Daishonin*, vol. I, p. 517.
3. Aristotle, *The Nicomachean Ethics*, Book III, ed. Lesley Brown, trans. David Ross (New York: Oxford University Press, 2009), p. 48.
4. *The Writings of Nichiren Daishonin*, vol. I, p. 4.
5. Keller, *Optimism: An Essay*, p. 67.
6. Ibid., 59.
7. Mihály Csikszentmihályi is noted for his work in the study of happiness and creativity and is best known for his book *Finding Flow: The Psychology of Engagement with Everyday Life*, in which he outlines his theory that people are happiest when they are in a optimal state of intrinsic motivation or complete absorption—that is, flow. As of 2012, he is Distinguished Professor of Psychology and Management at Claremont Graduate University and founding co-director of The Quality of Life Research Center, also at Claremont.
8. The Mystic Law is another name for Nam-myoho-renge-kyo, which is seen in Nichiren Buddhism as the universal law or principle. Nam-myoho-renge-kyo literally means devotion to Myoho-renge-kyo, which is the Japanese reading of the Chinese title of the Lotus Sutra.
9. Epictetus, *The Enchiridion*, in *The Works of Epictetus*, trans. Elizabeth Carter (London: F. C. and J. Rivington, 1807), p. 299.
10. *The Writings of Nichiren Daishonin*, vol. I, p. 637.
11. John Milton, *The Complete Poems of John Milton*, ed. Charles W. Eliot (New York: P. F. Collier & Son, 1909), p. 96.
12. *The Writings of Nichiren Daishonin*, vol. I, p. 216.
13. Keller, *Optimism: An Essay*, p. 17.
14. Lao Tzu, *Tao Te Ching*, trans. Stephen Mitchell (New York: HarperCollins Perennial Classics, 2000), Chapters 6, 35.

CONVERSATION FIVE
RECOVERING PURPOSE AND CONNECTION

1. Rabindranath Tagore, *The Religion of Man: Being the Hibbert Lectures for 1930* (New York: Macmillan, 1931), p. 13.
2. Konrad Lorenz, *On Aggression* (London: Routledge, 2002), p. 101.
3. Aristotle, *Politics*, trans. Benjamin Jowett, intr. H. W. C. Davis (Mineola, New York: Dover Publications, 2000), p. 29.

4. *The Writings of Nichiren Daishonin*, vol. II, p. 759.
5. Daisaku Ikeda, "Mahayana Buddhism and Twenty-first Century Civilization" in A New Humanism (London: I. B. Tauris, 2005), p. 167.
6. Daisaku Ikeda and Felix Unger, "The Humanist Principle—Compassion and Tolerance (2)" in *The Journal of Oriental Studies*, vol. 16 (October 2006), p. 34.
7. Norman Cousins, *The Healing Heart: Antidotes to Panic and Helplessness* (New York: W. W. Norton & Company, 1983), p. 102.
8. Doctors Without Borders is an international medical humanitarian organization created by doctors and journalists in France in 1971. Today, it provides independent, impartial assistance in more than 60 countries to people whose survival is threatened by violence, neglect, or catastrophe, primarily due to armed conflict, epidemics, malnutrition, exclusion from health care, or natural disasters. In 1999, Doctors Without Borders received the Nobel Peace Prize. (Source: Doctors Without Borders website: < http://www.doctorswithoutborders.org/ >)
9. Benjamin P. Kurtz, *The Pursuit of Death: A Study of Shelley's Poetry* (New York: Oxford University Press, 1933), p. 224.
10. Arnold Toynbee and Daisaku Ikeda, *Choose Life: A Dialogue* (London: I. B. Tauris, 2007), pp. 322, 342.

CONVERSATION SIX
ALL ARE WORTHY OF RESPECT

1. Martha Nussbaum, *The Therapy of Desire: Theory and Practice in Hellenistic Ethics* (Princeton: Princeton University Press, 1994), pp. 33–34.
2. *The Lotus Sutra and Its Opening and Closing Sutras*, trans. Burton Watson (Tokyo: Soka Gakkai, 2009), p. 272.
3. Lou Marinoff, *The Big Questions: How Philosophy Can Change Your Life*, p. 254.
4. *Kodomo no sekai* was published in 1998 and is available in Japanese, Russian, and Chinese.
5. *The Book of the Kindred Sayings (Samyutta Nikaya)*, ed. and trans. F. L. Woodward (London: The Pali Text Society, 1993), 3:8.
6. The phrase "tough love" was probably coined in 1968 with the publication of *Tough Love* by Bill Milliken. It described an approach used by many programs working with at-risk and challenging youth. In the late 1970s, David and Phyllis York of Pennsylvania launched a grass-roots support network for parents called Tough Love. By the early 1980s, it had more than 250 chapters across the United States and Canada, due in part to the recommendation of columnist Ann Landers. Tough Love parent support groups soon spread around the globe and continue to be active as of this writing. The Yorks published a bestseller, also called *Tough Love*, in 1985.
7. *The Complete Poetical Works of Lord Byron*, ed. Bliss Perry (Boston: Houghton Mifflin, 1905), p. 936.
8. Ralph Waldo Emerson, "The Conduct of Life," in *Essays and Lectures*, ed. Joel Porte (New York: Library of America, 1983), p. 1072.

CONVERSATION SEVEN
THE NATURE OF HEALING

1. Epicurus, "Fragments," no. 54, in *Epicurus, The Extant Remains*, trans. Cyril Bailey (Oxford: The Clarendon Press; 1926), p. 133.
2. World Health Organization fact sheet no. 220, September 2010 (http://www.who.int/mediacentre/factsheets/fs220/en/).
3. *New England Journal of Medicine*, July 26, vol. 357, no. 4.
4. *The Writings of Nichiren Daishonin*, vol. I, p. 614.
5. In 1901, Pablo Casals, then twenty-four years old, toured the United States with Madame Emma Nevada. On March 16, hiking with companions in the San Francisco area, he reports: "It was when we were making our descent on Mount Tamalpais that the accident occurred. Suddenly one of my companions shouted, 'Watch out, Pablo!' I looked up and saw a boulder hurtling down the mountainside directly toward me. I jerked my head aside and was lucky not to be killed. As it was, the boulder hit and smashed my left hand—my fingering hand. My friends were aghast. But when I looked at my mangled bloody fingers, I had a strangely different reaction. My first thought was 'Thank God, I'll never have to play the cello again!'" See Pablo Casals and Albert Eugene Kahn, *Joys and Sorrows* (New York: Simon & Schuster, 1970), p. 105.
6. *The Writings of Nichiren Daishonin*, vol. II, p. 668.
7. Lou Marinoff, *The Big Questions: How Philosophy Can Change Your Life*, p. xii.
8. *The Writings of Nichiren Daishonin*, vol. II, p. 1060.
9. John Dewey, *The Middle Works: 1899–1924*, vol. 2: 1902–1903, ed. Jo Ann Boydston (Carbondale: Southern Illinois University Press, 2008), p. 92.
10. *The Writings of Nichiren Daishonin*, vol. I, p. 629.

CONVERSATION EIGHT
HEALING THE WOUNDS OF ARBITRARY DIVISION

1. Rabindranath Tagore, *Towards Universal Man* (New York: Asia Publishing House, 1961), p. 234.
2. Three thousand realms in a single moment of life: A philosophical system established by Zhiyi in his *Great Concentration and Insight*. The number three thousand comes from the following calculation: 10 (Ten Worlds) x 10 (Ten Worlds) x 10 (ten factors) x 3 (three realms of existence). Life at any moment manifests one of the Ten Worlds. Each of these worlds possesses the potential for all ten within it, and this "mutual possession," or mutual inclusion, of the Ten Worlds is represented as a hundred possible worlds. Each of these hundred worlds possesses the ten factors, making one thousand factors, or potentials, and these operate within each of the three realms of existence, thus making three thousand realms. (Source: *The Soka Gakkai Dictionary of Buddhism*, pp. 686–88)
3. *The Writings of Nichiren Daishonin*, vol. II, p. 307.
4. Nichiren, *The Record of the Orally Transmitted Teachings*, pp. 211–12.

5. *The Writings of Nichiren Daishonin*, vol. I, p. 989.
6. Emerson, *Nature*, in *Essays and Lectures*, p. 47.
7. *The Journals and Miscellaneous Notebooks of Ralph Waldo Emerson*, eds. William H. Gilman, Ralph H. Orth, et al., 16 vols. (Cambridge: Harvard University Press, 1960–82), 5:18–19.
8. Henry David Thoreau, *Walden*, in *A Week, Walden, The Maine Woods, Cape Cod*, ed. Robert F. Sayre (New York: Library of America, 1985), p. 352.
9. Diogenes Laertius: "Life of Zenon," in *The Lives of the Philosophers*, Book VII, trans. C. D. Yonge, 1895. Accessed at < http://www.attalus.org/old/diogenes7a.html >.

CONVERSATION NINE
THE HEALING POWER OF DIALOGUE

1. Emerson, "Friendship," in *Essays and Lectures*, p. 339.
2. *The Lotus Sutra and Its Opening and Closing Sutras*, p. 308.
3. *The Writings of Nichiren Daishonin*, vol. II, p. 843.
4. Ibid., 57.
5. Ibid., 221.
6. Translated from Japanese. *Nitobe Inazo Zenshu* (The Complete Works of Nitobe Izano), vol. 20 (Tokyo: Kyobunkwan, 1987), pp. 44–62.

CONVERSATION TEN
DIALOGUE FOR PEACE AND HUMANISM

1. Walt Whitman, *Leaves of Grass*, in *Poetry and Prose*, ed. Justin Kaplan (New York: Library of America, 1982), p. 400.
2. Glenn Gould's performance of the Prelude and Fugue in C major from Book II of *The Well-Tempered Clavier* was chosen for inclusion on the NASA Voyager Golden Record by a committee headed by Carl Sagan. The disc of recordings was placed on the spacecraft *Voyager 1*, which is approaching interstellar space and is the farthest human-made object from Earth.
3. Dr. Ikeda has met with more than 7,000 world leaders and intellectuals and engaged in 1,600 dialogues with people, including the outstanding twentieth-century historian Arnold J. Toynbee.
4. Richard Nikolaus von Coudenhove-Kalergi (1894–1972) is recognized as the founder of the first popular movement for a united Europe. An Austrian politician and philosopher, he published the book *Pan-Europa* in 1923, and from April 1924 to March 1938, he worked as an editor and principal author of the journal *Paneuropa*. He continued to publish throughout his life.
5. Nichiren, *The Record of the Orally Transmitted Teachings*, p. 165.
6. Kaneko Ikeda, *Kaneko's Story* (Santa Monica, Calif.: World Tribune Press, 2008), p. 98.
7. *The Writings of Nichiren Daishonin*, vol. I, p. 6.
8. Ibid., 7.
9. *The Questions of King Milinda*, trans. T. W. Rhys Davids (Oxford: Clarendon Press, 1890), p. 46.

CONVERSATION ELEVEN
ANCIENT QUESTIONS, TIMELESS WISDOM

1. *Selections from the Meditations of Marcus Aurelius*, trans. Benjamin E. Smith (New York: Century, 1899), p. 28.
2. Seneca, "Dialogues and Essays," in *Oxford World Classics*, trans. John Davie (Oxford: Oxford University Press, 2007), p. 155.
3. *The Writings of Nichiren Daishonin*, vol. I, p. 1120.
4. Virtue, or *arête*, was a central concern not just of Socrates, but of all the philosophers of ancient Greece. Aristotle in particular devoted much reflection to understanding virtue. The Stanford Encyclopedia of Philosophy (online) states that Aristotle "distinguishes two kinds of virtue: those that pertain to the part of the soul that engages in reasoning (virtues of mind or intellect), and those that pertain to the part of the soul that cannot itself reason but is nonetheless capable of following reason (ethical virtues, virtues of character)." Aristotle's doctrine of the mean, which is explored in his *Nichomachean Ethics*, places virtue between the vices of deficiency and excess. For example, courage is located between the deficiency of fear and the excess of rash behavior.
5. The 34th G8 summit took place in Toyako, Japan, on the northern island of Hokkaido, July 7–9, 2008. Participants represented France, Germany, Italy, Japan, the United States, the United Kingdom, Canada, and Russia. Topics included the economy, global warming, and aid for Africa.
6. Toynbee and Ikeda, *Choose Life: A Dialogue*, p. 26.
7. Jan Smuts, *Holism and Evolution* (New York: The Macmillan Company, 1926).

CONVERSATION TWELVE
ON THE PRACTICE OF VIRTUE

1. The Japanese lunar calendar was based on the Chinese calendar. Each year started anywhere from about three to seven weeks later than the modern Gregorian year, so, while it is common practice, it is not entirely accurate to equate the first month with January.
2. Toynbee sent Ikeda the invitation on September 23, 1969.
3. *The Writings of Nichiren Daishonin*, vol. I, p. 23.
4. Ibid., 612.
5. Marcus Tullius Cicero, *The Orations of Marcus Tullius Cicero*, vol. II, trans. C. D. Yonge (London: Henry G. Bohn, 1852), p. 301.
6. *The Writings of Nichiren Daishonin*, vol. I, p. 302.
7. Ibid., 770.
8. Arnold Toynbee, *A Study of History*, abridged by D. C. Somervell (London: Oxford University Press, 1963), p. 255.
9. "The Maxims of Theognis," in *The Works of Hesiod, Callimachus, and Theognis*, trans. Rev. J. Banks (London: Henry G. Bohn, 1856), p. 225.
10. Daisaku Ikeda, *The Living Buddha*, trans. Burton Watson (Santa Monica, Calif.: Middleway Press, 2008), p. 135.
11. Marcus Aurelius, *Meditations*, trans. Maxwell Staniforth (London: Penguin Books, 1964), p. 157.

12. Lou Marinoff, *The Middle Way: Finding Happiness In a World of Extremes*, p. 39.
13. The eightfold path is an early teaching of Buddhism setting forth the principles to be followed in order to attain emancipation: 1) right views, 2) right thinking, 3) right speech, 4) right action, 5) right way of life, 6) right endeavor, 7) right mindfulness, and 8) right meditation.
14. The six *paramitas*, or perfections, are practices required of Mahayana bodhisattvas in order to attain Buddhahood: 1) almsgiving, 2) keeping the precepts, 3) forbearance, 4) assiduousness, 5) meditation, and 6) the obtaining of wisdom. (Source: *The Soka Gakkai Dictionary of Buddhism*, pp. 611–12)
15. Daisaku Ikeda, *The New Human Revolution*, vol. 21 (Santa Monica, Calif.: World Tribune Press, 2010), p. 33.

CONVERSATION THIRTEEN
THE ARTS AND THE HUMAN SPIRIT

1. *The Lotus Sutra and Its Opening and Closing Sutras*, p. 272.
2. *The Writings of Nichiren Daishonin*, vol. II, p. 186.
3. *I Ching* (Book of Changes), trans. Richard Wilhelm and Carey Baynes (Princeton, New Jersey: Princeton University Press, 1967), p. 68.
4. Ibid., 69.
5. The online mathematics resource WolframMathWorld says that the "golden ratio, also known as the divine proportion, golden mean, or golden section, is a number often encountered when taking the ratios of distances in simple geometric figures such as the pentagon, pentagram, decagon, and dodecahedron. It is denoted φ, or sometimes τ." The golden ratio is often associated visually with the golden rectangle and Fibonacci Spiral. For an extended discussion of the golden ratio in the context of Aristotelian philosophy and the iconography of wisdom traditions, see Lou Marinoff, *The Middle Way*, Chapter Two, "Aristotle's Golden Mean," and Chapter Five, "ABC Geometry."
6. *Nam-myoho-renge-kyo*: The ultimate law or truth of the universe, according to Nichiren's teachings. Nichiren identifies it with the universal law or principle implicit in the meaning of the Lotus Sutra. (Source: *The Soka Gakkai Dictionary of Buddhism*, p. 424)
7. *The Writings of Nichiren Daishonin*, vol. I, p. 3.
8. June 1992 *Seikyo Times*, p. 8.
9. Ibid., 15.
10. Ibid., 17.
11. *The Writings of Nichiren Daishonin*, vol. II, p. 204.
12. Makiguchi was imprisoned by Japanese authorities for his unwillingness to support the imperial Japanese government that had been consolidating its power since its full-scale invasion of China in 1937, and which culminated in the fighting of World War II. Specifically, Makiguchi and his protégé Josei Toda refused to abandon their pacifist convictions, recant their Buddhist practice in favor of state-sponsored Shintoism, and adhere to what the Tsunesaburo Makiguchi website (< http://www.tmakiguchi.org/ >) describes as "the cult of imperial divinity." Already in his 70s, Makiguchi died in prison in November 1944. Toda was released in July 1945.

13. Tagore, *Towards Universal Man*, p. 234.
14. *The Writings of Nichiren Daishonin*, vol. I, p. 258.

CONVERSATION FOURTEEN
LIFE AND DEATH ARE NOT SEPARATE

1. April 20, 2001, *World Tribune*, p. 6.
2. *Tao Te Ching*, Chapter 64.
3. Informally called the "happiness index," the Better Life Index, published by the Organisation for Economic Co-operation and Development (< http://www.oecd.org/ >) measures life satisfaction in 40 countries.
4. *The Writings of Nichiren Daishonin*, vol. I, p. 632.
5. Epicurus, "Letter to Menoeceus," in *The Extant Remains*, p. 85.
6. *The Lotus Sutra and Its Opening and Closing Sutras*, p. 271.
7. Martin Luther King, Jr., *A Testament of Hope: The Essential Writings and Speeches of Martin Luther King, Jr.*, ed. James M. Washington (New York: HarperCollins, 1991), p. 222.
8. For reports on this and related events, see the "Understanding Death, Appreciating Life" subsection of the Themes section of the Ikeda Center website, < http://www.ikedacenter.org/ >.
9. Michel de Montaigne, "That our happiness must not be judged until after our death," in *The Complete Essays of Michel de Montaigne*, trans. Donald M. Frame (Stanford, Calif.: Stanford University Press, 1957, 1965), p. 55.
10. Harvey G. Cox and Daisaku Ikeda, *The Persistence of Religion: Comparative Perspectives on Modern Spirituality* (London: I. B. Tauris, 2009).
11. Blaise Pascal, *Pensées*, trans. A. J. Krailsheimer (London: Penguin Classics, 1966, 1995), p. 51.
12. Daisaku Ikeda, *Songs from My Heart*, trans. Burton Watson (Tokyo: Weatherhill, 1978), p. 29.
13. Daisaku Ikeda, *The Human Revolution*, Book One (Santa Monica, Calif.: World Tribune Press, 2004), p. 228.
14. Translated from Japanese. Leo Tolstoy, *Torusutoi Zenshu* (Collected Works of Tolstoy) (Tokyo: Iwanami Shoten, 1931), vol. 21, p. 408.
15. Ikeda, *A New Humanism*, pp. 166–67.

CONVERSATION FIFTEEN
WOMEN AND THE BUILDING OF PEACE CULTURES

1. Martin Buber, *I and Thou*, trans. Walter Kaufmann (New York: Touchstone, 1996).
2. Ibid.
3. Simon Baron-Cohen, *The Essential Difference: Male and Female Brains and the Truth about Autism* (New York: Basic Books, 2003), pp. 21–22.
4. For example, see E. Maccoby and C. Jacklin, *The Psychology of Sex Differences* (Stanford, Calif.: Stanford University Press, 1975).
5. In his essay "The Moral Equivalent of War" (1906), James said that "military feelings are too deeply grounded to abdicate their place among our ideals until

better substitutes are offered." James envisioned a form of national service dedicated to improving human society through what he called the conquest of nature. This process would enable the "martial type of character" to be "bred without war," he wrote. Though not anticipated by James, modern sports competitions can be seen as serving a similar purpose.

6. Mahatma Gandhi, *All Men Are Brothers* (New York: Continuum, 2005), p. 162.

7. Margaret Mead, *Women at War—A Deadly Species* (Boulder, Colo.: Paladin Books, 1977), p. 6.

8. M. Binkin and S. Bach, *Women and the Military* (Washington, D.C.: The Brookings Institution, 1977), p. 134.

9. For an overview of Jiang Qing's actions, see "The 25 Most Powerful Women of the Past Century" at the Time Specials section of the *Time* magazine website (< http://www.time.com/time/specials/packages/article/0, 28804,2029774_20 29776_2031838,00.html >).

10. Daisaku Ikeda, "To the Young Mothers of Kosen-rufu," SGI-USA *Publications* 1997–2008 CD (Santa Monica, Calif.: World Tribune Press, 2009), Bonus Articles, p. 15. Also in the February 14, 2007, *Seikyo Shimbun* (Japanese).

11. For example, see "The Ethics of Care and Feminist Ethics," in *Biomedical Ethics*, eds. Thomas Mappes and David DeGrazia (New York: McGraw-Hill, 6th edition, 2006), pp. 30–33.

12. *The Writings of Nichiren Daishonin*, vol. I, p. 930.

13. In this story, the dragon king's daughter is the eight-year-old daughter of Sagara, one of the eight great dragon kings said to live at the bottom of the sea. The dragon kings were among those assembled at the gathering where Shakyamuni preached the Lotus Sutra. Despite her age, her gender, and the fact that she was an animal, the dragon king's daughter gained enlightenment after hearing Bodhisattva Manjushri preach the Lotus Sutra. Her enlightenment refutes the idea of the time that women could never attain enlightenment. It also reveals that the power of the Lotus Sutra enables all people equally to attain Buddhahood in their present form, without undergoing uncountable lifetimes of austere practices. See "Devadatta," in *The Lotus Sutra and Its Opening and Closing Sutras*, pp. 182–89.

CONVERSATION SIXTEEN
TO RELIEVE SUFFERING AND IMPART JOY

1. Aug. 1, 2003, *World Tribune*, p. 8.

2. *The Writings of Nichiren Daishonin*, vol. I, p. 79.

3. Ibid., 24.

4. Translated from Japanese. J. Takakusu, ed. *Nanden Daizokyo*, vol. 24 (Tokyo: Taisho Shinshu Daizokyo Publishing Society, 1935), p. 358.

5. Nichiren writes, "When one comes to realize and see that each thing—the cherry, the plum, the peach, the damson—in its own entity, without undergoing any change, possesses the eternally endowed three bodies, then this is what is meant by the word *ryo*, 'to include' or all-inclusive" (*The Record of the Orally Transmitted Teachings*, 200).

6. Toynbee and Ikeda, *Choose Life: A Dialogue*, p. 285.

Index

About the Authors

LOU MARINOFF is Professor and Chair of Philosophy at The City College of New York. He is also founding president of the American Philosophical Practitioners Association, and editor of its journal *Philosophical Practice*. Marinoff has authored internationally bestselling books (including *Plato Not Prozac!*, translated into twenty-seven languages) that apply philosophy to the resolution of everyday problems. He has collaborated with global think tanks and leadership forums such as the Aspen Institute, BioVision (Lyon), Festival of Thinkers (Abu Dhabi), Horasis (Zurich), Strategic Foresight Group (Mumbai), and the World Economic Forum (Davos). His dialogue with Daisaku Ikeda was published in Japan in 2011.

DAISAKU IKEDA is President of the Soka Gakkai International, a lay Buddhist organization with more than twelve million members worldwide. He has written and lectured widely on Buddhism, humanism, and global ethics. More than fifty of his dialogues have been published, including conversations with figures such as Mikhail Gorbachev, Hazel Henderson, Joseph Rotblat, Linus Pauling, and Arnold Toynbee. Dedicated to education promoting humanistic ideals, in 1971 President Ikeda founded Soka University in Tokyo and, in 2001, Soka University of America in Aliso Viejo, California.